PRIMARY SCIENCE

A Guide for Teachers

Romola Showell

Ward Lock Educational

© Romola Showell 1989
First published 1989

Ward Lock Educational,
T R House, Christopher Road, East Grinstead, Sussex RH19 3BT

A member of the Ling Kee Group
HONG KONG • TAIPEI • SINGAPORE • LONDON • NEW YORK

Front cover design by Cathy Gilmour

ISBN 0 7062 4995 X

British Library of Cataloguing in Publication Data

CONTENTS

Introduction   4

Suggested apparatus and equipment   6

1   Growing things   8
2   See how they grow   10
3   Room to grow   12
4   Looking at a tree   14
5   Life on earth   16
6   Insects   18
7   Other invertebrates   20
8   Small animals in the environment   22
9   Any small mammal   24
10   Shape and size   26
11   The next generation   28
12   Ourselves   30
13   Bones, skeletons and movement   32
14   Living in water   34
15   Moulds and other strange plants   36
16   Look at soil   38
17   Rocks   40
18   Fibres, yarns and fabrics   42
19   Water on tap   44
20   Metals all around   46
21   Sticking it together   48
22   Wheels   50
23   Tools and machines   52
24   Friction and movement   54
25   Stress, strain and structures   56
26   Bridges   58

27   Colours   60
28   Something about sound   62
29   Time things   64
30   Mathematics and nature   66
31   Keeping warm and keeping cool   68
32   Mirrors   70
33   Air is there   72
34   Wet weather   74
35   Sun and summer   76
36   As cold as ice   78
37   Hedges   80
38   Environmental factors – a look around   82
39   Exploring your own environment   84
40   Walls   86
41   Seashore and cliff   88
42   Town biology   90
43   Adaptation and variation   92
44   Conservation and pollution   94
45   Counting, sampling and solving   96
46   Making use of collections   98

A tree chart – project sheet   100
Environmental study project sheet   101
Bibliography   102
Index   103

INTRODUCTION

Science begins as soon as children start to look around and see all the interesting things there are – trees, animals, cars, walls, bridges, water, fire – the list goes on and on. It begins when they realize that liquids pour and that birds fly, and they want to know why. So it is sad that there are still primary teachers who, because of their own limited knowledge, feel nervous about teaching science. Those who did not enjoy it when they were at school often have rather hazy recollections of complicated physics and chemistry experiments, and feel inadequately prepared for successfully developing the subject in the classroom. However, the willing teacher can learn along with the children and, in any case, almost all teachers are actually doing science without necessarily realizing it.

Science learning must start in the infant classes and continue all through the primary years so that a background of sound knowledge is acquired and children know *how* to look, as well as *where* to look. Science needs to be formalized to some extent because science is an exact study – even for the youngest children – and all work, however elementary, must have an aim and a reasonable outcome. At the end of any project, something new should have been learned.

In the primary school, science should be a highly practical subject in which children learn to observe accurately, to devise experiments in order to find the answer to problems, and to record what they have found out in a scientific manner, however simply. As they get older, they will begin to develop the ability to communicate their findings to others and to make reasoned deductions from the results of their investigations. The scope for the primary child is vast. If presented properly, these early lessons will form the basis for the more advanced work in the secondary school. Indeed, it is in the primary classroom that the beginnings of a permanent interest may take root.

This book is intended for any primary teacher who wants some ideas for starting science or for class projects. It is not intended to be an overall syllabus nor to cover all possible areas. Rather it presents a series of topics which could be used, with adaptation, for primary children of any age. Some of them are obviously more suitable for the older or younger child, but I have made no attempt to divide them into such categories as 'infant' or 'older juniors'. This is a book to dip into and use as it suits. The ideas are all mine – those that I have found to be successful – but there are many more which teachers can work out for themselves, and which may be better for their own classroom. I hope that, after trying out some activities in this book, teachers will be able to appreciate the elements of science in much of the work that is already carried out in the school, and will be able to make the best use of opportunities as they arise.

Some primary schools may already have an established science syllabus. If so, many of the suggested themes will fit in with this or augment it with a new approach. For teachers who feel that all subjects should be integrated, I think they will see how science links with many of the other subjects found in the normal curriculum.

General notes

1 Traditionally, science in schools has been divided into biology, chemistry and physics, but this is too structured for primary children. The topics in this book contain elements of these subjects, but they also include mathematics, geology and environmental studies.

2 All science should be practical, and should be introduced in such a way that children can see *why* they are doing experiments and making observations. No two teachers will work in the same way. It is up to each one to decide whether the work should be done by the whole class or as a group activity; but however it is organized it can reasonably be divided into:
a) Introduction by means of a talk, a demonstration, a visit, a particular event, a study of specimens, etc.
b) Discussion with the children to decide how the work will be carried out
c) Organization of necessary resources or activities, with detailed planning of the topic: time scale; class or group activities; the work of each group or child; anticipated outcome
d) Doing the work
e) Recording what has been done or seen
f) Putting the work together and displaying it as a whole
g) Evaluation of the whole project, and retention for future reference

3 The recording of the work is essential if science, as a primary subject, is to be treated seriously. The method will vary according to age, ability, and the requirements of the teacher, but it must be done in some way. Here are a few suggestions:
a) Talking – the child talking to the teacher, to a group or to the class; or using a tape recorder
b) Writing – from a single word caption to a full description; or a series of ordered notes
c) Graphic and three-dimensional presentation – painting, modelling, drawing, tabulating and charting
d) Photography
e) Demonstration – for example, making a windmill or a water wheel; or explaining how one is made
f) Annotation – of collections of specimens, or a series of experiments

4 It is worth keeping individual and group topic books as part of the class library. They are often useful, particularly if they include lists of the reference books used.

Apparatus and equipment

Despite problems of storage and lack of work space, science can be taught in the everyday classroom by keeping resources within reasonable limits. I have kept suggestions for expensive apparatus to an absolute minimum. This is purely for economic reasons and not because there is any particular merit in using home-made materials. It is, however, perfectly possible to use many cheap or throw-away items without any detriment to the work. Any money available can then be used for buying good reference books and apparatus for which there is no adequate substitute such as hand lenses, microscopes, accurate timers, mirrors. See the list of suggested apparatus at the end of this section.

Books and other resources

The use of workcards and worksheets is the choice of the individual teacher but, if the work is well planned and the children know exactly what is expected of them, they should not be necessary. If used they should be made for the particular group in mind; be well thought out and well presented; not be too limiting; above all, not be used instead of practical work and first-hand observation.

Reference books – as many as possible – will be needed. These should be both accurate and readable. Even books far beyond the ability of the age group are valuable because of their illustrations and extra information. They can be used with the help of the teacher or other adult.

The use of all available resources makes the teaching of science much more absorbing. Some of the less obvious possibilities are as follows:

a) Comics, pamphlets, brochures, newspapers, catalogues, magazines – the ability to use sources of information other than reference books is needed for any subject

b) Objects – any items that can be used to exploit scientific ideas, such as a bicycle; mechanical toys; collections of rocks or metals, natural specimens

c) People – experts with specialized knowledge or skills; craftspeople and technicians

d) Audio-visual facilities – slides, films, film strips, video tapes, television, radio, photographs

e) Places – museums, zoos, safari parks, parks, nature trails, historical sites, workshops and natural sites such as woodland, seashore, hedgerow, pond

f) Special sources of information – Nature Conservancy Council, Royal Society for the Protection of Birds, Forestry Commission, for example.

Primary children are enthusiastic and work that interests and stimulates them will produce the best results. Whatever work they do should be worthwhile and with a definite aim in mind, and whatever information they are given should be accurate. If you don't know the answer, admit it and make use of the reference books to find it or, better still, devise some work so that you and the children can find out together. The teacher who is really interested is much more likely to encourage the children to look, find out, and to assess. The children should not only learn about the world in which they live, but they should also enjoy the processes by which they acquire their knowledge. They are inquisitive, too, so now is the time to help them find the answers to all those questions they keep on asking. Why doesn't a duck get wet? What would happen if wheels were square? How does a fish breathe? Why do some things float? What's a caterpillar? Look for answers, talk about them – and remember that science starts at the very beginning. So make it exciting for all the children you teach.

Some of this apparatus and equipment will be found in any school and much of it can be collected quite easily, but some items will have to be purchased if not already available. Some are desirable but not essential. The animal inspection cages, seed propagator and mouse/hamster cage could be made reasonably cheaply.

Easily collected apparatus
Plastic bottles, pots, jars
Metal foil
String, tape, rubber bands
Matchboxes and other boxes
Garden canes
Tins (if ends need to be removed, do so with a rotary opener so that there are no sharp edges)
Balloons
Plastic bags
Adhesive tape
Corks
Bricks
Toys
Plastic sweet jars
Wire
Saucers

School apparatus
Modelling clay
Scissors
Scales and balances
Rulers and tape measures
Crayons and paints
Timers (simple sand timers and an easily seen stop clock)
Measuring jugs and beakers

Purchased apparatus
Good glass hand lenses
Mirrors
Balance with deep pans
Plastic tubing
Building toys (Lego, etc.)
Plastic washing up bowls
Magnets
Candles
Plastic trays
Plastic buckets
Thermometers (room, clinical and soil)
Plastic funnels
Aquarium tanks (several small ones are better than one large one; a large full tank is immovable)
Tweezers
Strong plastic boxes with lids

Desirable but not essential apparatus
Binocular microscope
Mouse/hamster cage
Tape recorder
Slide viewers
Gardening tools
Perspex sheets
Animal inspection cage
Seed propagator
Slide and film strip projector
Camera
Thick plastic sheeting

For some sections, special apparatus will be needed (spindles; insect cages; electric iron; vacuum flask, for example) but these are normally easy to borrow or make.

Tools
Hammer
Nails
Pliers
Flower pots
Seed trays
Hand fork
Trowel
Needles
Spoons
Screwdrivers
Screws
Indoor watering can
Small saw
Electric kettle (for teacher's use when warm water is needed)

1 GROWING THINGS

The growing of plants will only be interesting for children if it is made interesting. Children like instant results and they cannot be expected to follow the slow progress of growth without some sort of stimulus. It helps if they are given some understanding of the life cycle of plants.

General Notes

1 Living things grow, and increase in size is a sign of growth. Animals tend to grow to a definite size and shape within a limited time, but plants grow throughout their lives and the amount of growth varies considerably. Plants range from minute to enormous: the most massive living thing on earth is the giant Wellingtonia (Sequoia).

2 Growth is affected by the immediate environment, and the habitat of one plant may be completely unsuitable for another. Basically, plants need water, air, light and a particular temperature if they are to grow properly. Children can experiment with growing seeds, in different conditions. For example, using mustard seeds:
a) Those *without water* will not start to grow at all
b) Those *in a very cold temperature* will grow only very slowly (or not at all if it is too cold)
c) Those grown *in the dark* will be tall, spindly and yellow, eventually dying

3 Green plants need light if they are to grow properly. Plants build up their food from the elements in water and air. In order to do this they need light energy, and this can only be used in the presence of the green colouring found in leaves (chlorophyll). Non-green plants (fungi, moulds, etc.) cannot build up food and so have to take food from other living or dead plant material. Some leaves do not appear to be green (e.g. Copper Beech) but the leaves do contain chlorophyll.

4 Children are familiar with the fact that plants can be grown from seed, and they should see as many seeds as possible, but they should also look at vegetative reproduction:
a) Bulbs and corms – onion, daffodil, crocus
b) Tubers – potato, dahlia
c) Runners – couch grass, strawberry
d) Leaf and stem cuttings, root division, grafting – methods used by gardeners

5 Other interesting features of plant growth are:
a) Climbing plants – the ways in which stems spiral (and the direction of the spirals); tendrils; the ways in which plants cling to trees and brickwork
b) Reaction of plants to stimuli – leaf movement towards light; root movement towards water and darkness

Activities and experiments

1 Growing plants from seed – children should prepare their own pots, plant the seeds, write the labels (with help if too young), and care for them. Seeds can be grown in ordinary soil or potting compost, and can be put into flower pots, yoghurt pots, etc. For speedy growth, mustard is probably the best (seeds scattered on the top of damp soil will germinate in a day or two). Other fast growers are radishes, lettuce, grass, peas, beans and tomatoes.

   Children can also try some of the more interesting or unusual seeds like maize, castor oil, wheat, marrow, peanut, apple, orange, acorn, horse chestnut, dandelion and birdseed. Plum, date and avocado are also interesting, but take a very long time to germinate.

Beans growing in a jar. Fill the centre with soil or sand so the blotting paper or paper towel won't tear

2 Seeds can be planted in a variety of ways:

a) On damp sawdust, cloth or sponge. Mustard is good for this method, but dishes dry out very quickly and seedlings often die in hot weather.

b) In egg shells. If the shells are filled with soil and faces painted on them, grass 'hair' can be grown. Suitable for the youngest children.

c) In a plastic bottle with the top cut off (safer than a glass jar). Use peas or beans in order to see all the stages of growth.

d) On the top of a bottle filled with water: suitable for acorns and other larger seeds. Make sure that the water reaches the seed. Bulbs can also be grown on the top of jars (an onion will grow in this way).

e) In a 'mini-greenhouse' made with a plastic bag and a rubber band. After the seeds have been planted in a flower pot, water well and put a small plastic bag over the top so that it sticks up to make a domed covering. Secure with a rubber band. Water condensing on the bag will run down into the pot, so more watering should not be needed before shoots appear.

3 A plant's response to light can be shown using a healthy green plant in a pot inside a cardboard box with a lid (a shoe box will do for a small plant). Make a hole (about the size of a 50p piece) in the middle of one end of the box. Put the plant in the box, at the opposite end, and put on the lid. Keep the box in the same position with the hole facing a source of light. If the box is only opened for watering, the leaves will bend towards the light hole. If a plant such as a pea is used, it can be left until the shoot eventually appears through the hole.

4 Give children the chance to see plants that they might otherwise not see – many city children are amazingly ignorant about food plants. Grow potatoes in large flower pots. One tuber will produce a large plant and the potatoes can be seen growing on their underground stems when the potato is dug up. A marrow or courgette can be grown in the same way, and peas or beans should be planted and kept until the pods form so that the children can see how the edible seeds are formed.

A visit to a botanical garden provides the opportunity to show more exotic plants such as tea, coffee, cotton.

5 With the youngest children, a class book can be made explaining what has been happening. The children can provide the pictures, and brief texts can be added: 'Today we planted our seeds'; 'Martin's seeds have started to grow'.

Older children can provide more detail, and a germination and growth chart can be filled in.

6 Children can make scrap books of plants in different categories (seed catalogues are useful for this). For example, 'Plants that feed us'; 'Cereals'; 'Useful plants' (jute, cotton, flax); 'Unusual plants' (seaweeds, cacti, fungi).

Seed growth chart

Date seeds were planted			
Seed	Date shoot appeared	Number of days since planted	Name of grower

Useful apparatus

Flower pots or any small plastic pots; small trowels and spoons; seed trays; hand lenses; plastic bags; rubber bands; potting compost; plastic drinks bottles; old saucers; pieces of sponge; shoe boxes; watering can

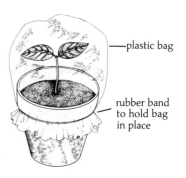

plastic bag

rubber band to hold bag in place

A mini-greenhouse

Young children can be introduced to the fact that growth and change are characteristic of living things, and that, in some cases, the changes can be so remarkable that the baby bears little resemblance to the adult (tadpole to frog; caterpillar to moth). Children soon realize that plants grow from seeds and that birds hatch from eggs. They can be shown other ways that animals reproduce – frog spawn and insect eggs, for example, and can be told that some baby animals, notably the mammals, grow inside the mother until ready to be born. Better still, they can share the excitement of waiting for the baby rabbits or guinea pigs to be born.

The common frog. The young of the frog – the tadpole – is unlike the adult

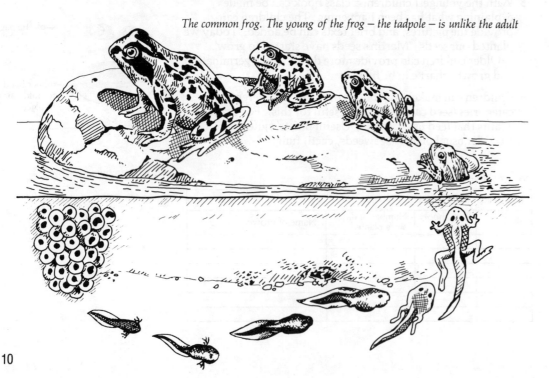

General notes

1 Animals grow to a definite size and shape according to their species, so a mouse will never grow as large as an elephant, and a cat will not have the neck of a giraffe. Once the full size is reached – and the time taken to do this varies considerably – variations will be slight, depending basically on the food supply. Length of life also varies. Human beings are the longest living animals, with a lifespan sometimes of over 100 years.

2 Animals need food for growth, energy and replacement of tissue. The natural food depends on the type of animal, but all animals – even the carnivores – depend on plants for food:

Food chains
Plankton → → → Small crustacea → → → Herring → → → Human beings
Wheat seed → → → Field mouse → → → Owl
Grass → → → Rabbit → → → Fox

3 Baby mammals resemble the adults, and growth changes involve increase in size and weight, development of skin covering and changes in the teeth. Baby birds may not look exactly like the parent, but there is no doubt that they are birds. This does not apply to the young of non-mammals such as the frog, newt and many of the insects whose adults look quite unlike the infants.

4 The life cycle of the frog will provide an example of an animal undergoing a complete change:

Eggs → → → Larval stage → → → → → → Frog
(Spawn)   (Tadpole)   gradual change

Tadpoles are easy to keep in the classroom, but conservation should be taught from an early stage and only a small quantity of spawn should be taken from any pond. A small tank can be used, with the bottom covered with sand and small stones and with water-weed planted in small pots. If a tank is unavailable, one or two tadpoles can be kept in a large jar. At first the newly hatched tadpoles feed on the spawn jelly, and then on weed and algae. As soon as the front legs grow, the tadpoles need to be able to get out of the water, and will need a large stone or floating raft. Once they are completely changed, they should be returned to a suitable pond because adult frogs are not easy to keep in captivity. For a different life cycle, see section 6 – Insects.

5 Guinea pigs are ideal for children to study because they can be watched and weighed within a few hours of birth. They are born furred, with their eyes open, and will run around the cage when only a few days old. Like all pets, they must be cared for properly (see section 9), and they can be watched and records kept of growth, food intake, etc.

Activities and experiments

1 Give children the opportunity to see as many animals as possible, both at the infant and adult stage. It is important to remember that when children use the word 'animal', they usually mean 'mammal', but biologically the word has a much wider meaning, and includes all living things not classified as plants.

  Human babies should not be forgotten. One of the children's mothers could probably be persuaded to bring a new baby into the classroom, and to talk about the infant.

2 Plan a zoo visit to see reptiles, fish and birds as well as mammals.

3 Use an ordinary hen's egg to see its structure.

4 Keep tadpoles, snails, water snails, caterpillars, stick insects, woodlice, etc.

5 Keep weight and length charts of an easily accessible baby animal.

  Note If animals are kept in school, they should be cared for properly with adequate provision for care during weekends and holiday time. If this is not possible, then keep them in the classroom for a short time only.

6 Plan studies of animals in specified groupings: pet animals; farm animals; pest animals; very small animals; flying animals, etc.

7 Find out about the growth rate and life span of different animals, and make a chart of the information. Other information could be added, such as size when fully grown, food, natural habitat.

Useful apparatus

Plastic sweet jars, with a piece of material fastened by a rubber band instead of a lid, make good containers for caterpillars etc.; balances with deep pans; personal scales; tape measures, hand lenses; camera; observation cage (for short time use only); animal cages (if animals are to be kept permanently); small shovel scraper and bucket for cleaning out cages

A mini-tank (large jam jar) for one or two tadpoles or water snails

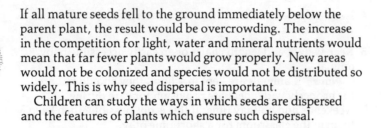

If all mature seeds fell to the ground immediately below the parent plant, the result would be overcrowding. The increase in the competition for light, water and mineral nutrients would mean that far fewer plants would grow properly. New areas would not be colonized and species would not be distributed so widely. This is why seed dispersal is important.

Children can study the ways in which seeds are dispersed and the features of plants which ensure such dispersal.

General notes

1 Many adaptations of plants enable seeds to be dispersed by either wind or animals. Some plants have explosive pods or capsules which propel the seeds away from the main plant, while others are adapted for water dispersal.

a) Wind dispersal

1 Fruits and seeds with 'parachutes' – willow-herb, dandelion, thistle, groundsel. These are light and easily moved by wind, often over very great distances.
2 Winged fruits – lime, sycamore, ash. The wing-like structures cause the fruits to spin as they fall from the tree, and increase their chance of being caught in an air current and carried further away.
3 Very light seeds – grasses.

4 Swaying stems – poppy, campion, snapdragon. The ripe fruit capsule develops one or more holes, through which the small seeds escape as the long flower stem is moved by the wind.

b) Animal dispersal

1 Hooked fruits – burdock, goosegrass. The outsides of these fruits have hook-like projections that catch on the fur of a passing animal.
2 Birds carry fruits away to eat them and many of these are dropped. Some hard or waxy seeds pass through the birds' digestive tract and are present in droppings.
3 Most animals assist with dispersal. They may knock against plants or carry small seeds on their feet. Children may not realize that even they are agents of dispersal, carrying and throwing such seeds as acorns and 'conkers'.

c) Explosive fruit dispersal

Broom, lupin, gorse. The pods split suddenly and with sufficient force to expel the seeds. (On a hot day the pods of broom or gorse can be heard splitting open).

d) Water dispersal

The interesting dispersal of coconuts can be discussed. Try to show the class a coconut with the fibre covering still intact.

2 Growth from seed is not the only way in which plants reproduce. Vegetative methods are equally important (see section 1) and can often ensure that plants spread rapidly over a large area. For example, the stolons of bramble; here very long stems grow out, bend over to touch the ground and the tips take root – often several feet away from the parent plant.

How would these seeds be dispersed?

Activities and experiments

1 Collecting – make collections of seeds, arranging them into sets according to their more obvious method of dispersal. Lids of shoe boxes, covered with cling film, make good display trays.

2 Problem solving – find out, by investigation, whether the size of a seed (or fruit) and the method of dispersal are related. Is it true that plants with large seeds tend to produce fewer than those with small seeds? Study wind dispersed seeds. How far can they travel from the parent plant? Look at plants growing in unusual places (on chimneys, in cracks in pavements). How did the seeds get there?

3 Efficiency test – of the seeds which are adapted for dispersal by animals (burdock or goose grass, for example) test how well these seeds stick to hair, fur, skin, feathers, sheeps' wool, etc. Try to find a tree (oak, beech, sycamore) growing in reasonable isolation. Look for seeds and seedlings underneath and around. Will these be able to grow properly? What will help the species to spread to new areas?

4 Importance of dispersal – do plants need room to grow? What are the results of overcrowding? Looking at an old hedge, the children can see how all the plants grow so that their leaves obtain adequate light. Plant mustard seeds in two pots of soil, scattering the seeds sparingly on the top of the soil in one and covering the soil thickly in the other. If both pots are kept watered and placed in a warm light place, the development of the plants can be compared.

5 Area study – make a study of a particular area and the plants found in it. If possible, compare this with other areas. For example, will willow-herb or dandelion grow anywhere? Look at a garden. Which plants are growing naturally and which have been put there?

Useful apparatus

Tape measures; plant pots; hand lenses; boxes and plastic bags for collecting; cling film and boxes for displays; seconds timer; camera

Many seeds are carried by sheep in their wool – grass seeds and hooked seeds like burdock

13

Sycamore

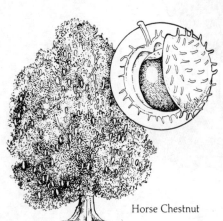

Horse Chestnut

Trees can be found almost anywhere, and a single tree can provide the basis for a project. Looking at trees in general is too big a topic for the youngest children; they will find it difficult to remember the characteristics of different species, and need to be able to read fluently if they are to identify even the commonest species from a book. Older children can make surveys, compare types and start to classify in various ways. It is, however, never too early to introduce children to tree studies, and to the care and conservation of trees.

If a tree is also introduced as a habitat for other living things, then it is likely to prove particularly interesting. Any tree can be looked at – even if the only one available is a badly trimmed plane or lime growing alongside a pavement. An old oak, horse chestnut or beech is the best. There are many things to be learned from trees in towns, and such a study could be the prelude to park, garden or woodland visits.

General notes

1 Children recognize trees from a very early age, but they seldom realize that they are plants and have the characteristics of plants. They are woody perennials with a single stem (or trunk) which may divide close to the ground. The flowers of trees are very varied and may be spectacular, like the horse chestnut, or fairly inconspicuous, like the ash. The children may already know what the blossom of apples, pears and plums looks like. In some species there are separate male flowers and female flowers, sometimes growing on different trees, e.g. willow and holly.

2 Trees reach a maximum height and spread and then stop growing, but the circumference of the trunk and branches increases, however slightly, during every year that the tree is alive. Children are often interested in such facts about trees as:

Oak wood is very hard and strong and will last a very long time. Oak trees produce their best timber when they are over 150 years old. They do not even produce acorns until they are about 60 years old.

The Wellingtonia is the largest growing plant in the world. In its native California it can grow over 100 m tall. In the Sequoia National Park there are specimens with a girth of over 27 m and with bark more than 0.5 m thick. They can live well over 3000 years.

The word 'beam' is the Anglo-Saxon word for tree – hence whitebeam and hornbeam.

3 Trees can be grouped as:
a) Broad leaved – lime, beech, oak, horse chestnut, plane are some. Most shed their leaves in autumn (holly is an exception).
b) Narrow leaved – pine, yew, cypress are examples. Most of these are evergreens (larch is an exception).

4 In young trees the bark is usually thin and smooth, but this gets thicker and more ridged with age. Each tree has its own characteristic wood and bark, and different woods have different uses.

5 Usually the roots of trees spread out as far underground as the branches spread above ground. Some roots penetrate deep into the sub-soil and basic rock. This is necessary both for anchorage and obtaining water.

6 Don't try any tree studies without a good basic book. *A Field Guide to the Trees of Britain and Northern Europe* by Alan Mitchell is recommended.

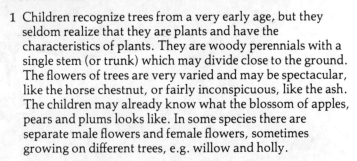

Activities and experiments

1 Use the Tree chart at the end of the book to start a study of a single tree. First look at the tree as a whole, then make various measurements (which older children can do themselves) – girth (officially measured at 1.5 m from the ground); height (estimated by comparison with the height of one of the children); leaf size (use squared paper); area of ground overshadowed by the branches.

2 Look in more detail at:
 a) Bark – texture, thickness, colour, pattern. Make bark rubbings
 b) Leaves – shape, size, colour and whether single or compound
 c) Flowers, fruits and seeds according to season
 d) Whether deciduous (losing their leaves in autumn) or coniferous

Coniferous and other evergreen trees also drop their leaves, but do so all the year round so that they are not leafless in winter.

3 Notice if there are other plants associated with the tree. There is often green alga on the trunk, which indicates the direction of prevailing rainfall because it grows on the wettest side of the trunk. Mistletoe may be found on some trees. This is a semi-parasitic plant which grows only on living trees. Different types of fungi can also be found, but many of these will also grow on dead and rotting trees.
 (Some fungi are poisonous, so don't let children handle them). Look at the plants under the tree. Vegetation will vary according to the type of tree (very little grows under pine trees, for example). Children can look at the effects of growing in shade and places where rain does not easily penetrate.

4 Look at animals associated with the tree:
 a) Birds feeding or nesting. Look for owl pellets
 b) Squirrels feeding or nesting. Rabbit droppings under the tree
 c) Insects feeding on the leaves. Look for caterpillars; insects and spiders on and under the bark
 d) Woodlice, centipedes, etc. in the litter under the tree

5 The possibilities for projects and displays are numerous and can be varied according to the age of the children. Infants can stick pictures of all they have found on a large cut out of the tree studied. Older children can make very detailed tree counts of a particular area. Other projects could follow on. For example, the use of timber both historically (oak ships and timber framed houses) and at the present time.

Useful apparatus

Flower pots; wax crayons; hand lenses; collecting boxes; nylon mesh bags; string; tape measures; squared paper; pieces of old sheet (for collecting specimens which fall from shaken branches)

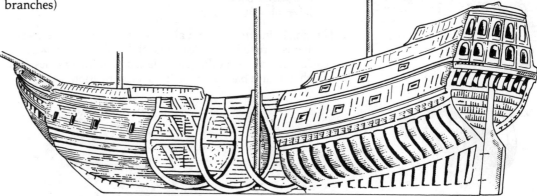

The English used to build their ships from oak. It could take 700 trees to build a large warship. So many trees were cut down that laws were passed 400 years ago to protect them. The oak forests have never been replaced.

15

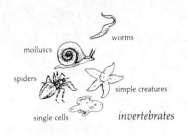

worms

molluscs

spiders

simple creatures

single cells

invertebrates

vertebrates

fish

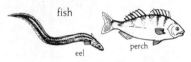

eel

perch

amphibians

frog

newt

reptiles

snake

tortoise

birds

swan

ostrich

mammals

squirrel

fox

Classification is the arrangement into groups or sets of any collection of similar things. This may sound too complex for children of primary age, but a simple classification of living things will serve to show them the vast variety of life on earth. It does not have to be detailed, and most children are used to sorting into size, colour, shape, etc., so they are not being faced with something entirely new.

Older children in particular seem to enjoy the discovery that every single living organism (of which well over a million have been named) fits into a pattern and has its particular characteristics.

General notes

1 No one really knows how many living organisms there actually are, but it is estimated that the numbers of different kinds are something like this:

Insects – about 1 million
Other invertebrates – about 950,000
Plants – about 335,000
Birds – over 8500
Mammals – about 5000

2 Naming living things is not always easy, and because every teacher is sure to have at least one child in each class who has read a book or been told about plant and animal names, it is worth having a basic knowledge of classification. Many things have common names (blackbird, lion, frog, oak), but they also have scientific names. The genus tells which group the organism belongs to (for example, *Panthera* includes lions, tigers, leopards and jaguars), and the species tells exactly what it is (*Panthera leo* is the lion). It is possible to classify much more fully by including family, order, class, phylum and kingdom, but this is beyond the grasp of children.

3 With the children, start by classifying some of the commoner animals. They should look at as many examples as possible so that they can see the differences for themselves.

Look first at the group called vertebrates (those having backbones).

4 Having learned about vertebrates, look at some of the other classifications, breaking them down into workable components (as above).

a) Invertebrates
See also section 7.
Worms
Coelenterates – examples, sea anenome, jelly fish
Molluscs – examples, slug, snail, oyster, squid
Arthropods (with jointed legs)
Many legged –examples, woodlouse, shrimp, centipede
Eight legged – examples, spider, harvestman
Six legged – examples, insect (see section 6)

b) Warm- or cold-blooded animals
Warm-blooded animals have a body temperature independent of that of the surrounding environment. This means that their temperature in cold weather is greater than that of the air around them. Cold-blooded animals have a body temperature which changes according to that of their environment.

16

c) Animals that fly
This will include birds, insects and bats. (Peculiarities such as 'flying' fish or 'flying' foxes interest children)

5 Plants can also be divided into groups but the plant kingdom is more difficult for children. It is probably better, in most cases, to classify according to habitat.

Some plant families have very definite characteristics, and it is easy to make a collection and to see the variation in both species and habitat. A good example is the daisy family (Compositae).

Activities and experiments

1 Following a zoo visit or a field trip, discuss all the animals and/or plants seen and classify them according to pre-determined groups. Make a card index with each species having its own card. This can be used as a reference for other topics.

2 When it is not possible to make visits or to catch small samples, some of this work can be done with good pictures, slides, film strips and films. Using these, get children to work out the characteristics of, say, amphibians and birds. For example:
a) Amphibians – young are unlike the adults (tadpoles); adults can live on land; lay eggs; usually have smooth moist skin; cold-blooded; vertebrate
b) Birds – possess feathers; warm-blooded; have two legs and two wings; most can fly; have a beak (no teeth); lay eggs; vertebrate

3 Make plant collections and classify in various ways:
Plants that grow in woodland; in towns; on cliffs, etc.
Plants of one family
Plants that can be classified as weeds
Plants found in books and then given both their common and scientific names (It is interesting to try to list all the common names used)

Children can be taught how to collect properly without damaging plants and without taking any rare species.

Useful apparatus

Good reference books; pots, bags and boxes for collecting; binoculars; pictures, slides and film strips

side 1   side 2

Ladybird

This is a beetle.
Number of legs – 6.
Wing cases – Yes. Red with
   7 spots.
Wings – Yes.
Where found – on
   dandelion.
Size – 8 mm.
Food – greenfly

Example of a file index card

6 INSECTS

Insects make up about 80% of known animals and are the most numerous species in the world. So it is not difficult to find suitable specimens for first hand observation. No other group is so varied in structure and habitat as the insects, and they can exist in vast numbers in a relatively small area (think of an ant hill). They can be found almost anywhere from the arctic to the tropics and are important as pests and spreaders of disease as well as pollinators.

While there are many examples that can be studied from life, there are some that can only be introduced through books, slides and film. It is important, then, that children first look at the familiar and learn as much as possible from specimens they can keep or can watch in their natural environment. After this, they can learn more about such less familiar insects as the locust, the tsetse fly, the colorado beetle and the praying mantis.

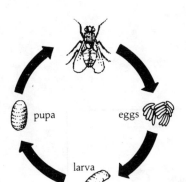

The life cycle of the house fly

General notes

1 Insects are found in every part of the world, and there are more than 20,000 species in the British Isles alone.

2 All insects have six legs, and this is the most easily recognized, distinguishing feature. The body of an insect is divided into three parts – the head, the thorax and the abdomen. The eyes are compound. Three pairs of jointed legs and the wings are attached to the thorax. Not all insects have wings, but most have one or two pairs. They usually have a pair of antennae.

3 Most insects pass through four stages of life:

Egg → → → larva → → → pupa → → → adult
           (caterpillar,   (chrysalis)   (imago)
           grub, maggot)

The butterfly, moth and housefly are examples. Some insects do not have a pupal stage. These include the stick insect, earwig, mosquito, ladybird.

Egg → → → larva → → → adult

4 Only the larva of an insect grows, and this moults several times during growth. Some insects spend their larval stage in water (gnat, dragon fly) and some insects spend most of their lives in water (most of the water beetles).

5 Insects feed by either biting their food (e.g. locusts and ants) or by sucking up liquid food (e.g. butterflies, houseflies and aphids).

6 Some species of insects form colonies. These are the so-called social insects and include ants and some bees and wasps.

7 Detailed classification of insects is too complicated for young children, but they will find it easier if they learn some of the characteristics of the major groups. These could be:

Butterflies and moths – most children find caterpillars and chrysalises from time to time
Flies – particularly houseflies
Beetles
Ants, wasps and bees
Grasshoppers and crickets
Fleas and lice – parasitic insects

Activities and experiments

1 Insects can be kept quite easily, and it is worthwhile taking the trouble to do this so that the children can watch them develop. The easiest to keep are the caterpillars of butterflies and moths. See that the children understand that caterpillars will only feed on their own particular food plants, so that if they find a caterpillar they must bring a leaf of the plant on which they found it.

If caterpillars are to be kept, they need proper conditions and housing to survive. Large plastic sweet jars, which are easily obtainable, can be used very successfully.

To keep the food plant fresh, put the stems in a small jar of water and put a strip of cotton wool round the top of the jar to prevent small caterpillars from falling into the water. Collapsible cages can be made using two equal sized lids and a piece of rolled acetate sheet. Roll the acetate sheet so that it will fit into one of the lids, and stick down the edge with adhesive tape. Perforate the other lid and use it for the top. The advantage of this cage is that it can be dismantled for storage. A thick layer of damp soil should be put in the bottom of each cage for those caterpillars which pupate underground, and a small piece of bark or wood for those which normally cling to a fence or tree trunk.

2 The common stick insects kept in many schools are natives of India. They are stick-like wingless insects with six long legs. They feed on privet and will moult several times before they are fully grown. The insects (which are bisexual) will each lay up to 500 eggs during a lifetime. The eggs laid in the autumn will hatch the following spring, and the insects live for several months. These can be kept in a large jar, like the caterpillars, or the children can be helped to make cages for them out of shoe boxes. Cut a large rectangle from a shoe-box lid and tape cellophane over this to make an observation window. Air holes can be punched in the sides of the box, and the food plant can be kept fresh by putting it in a small jar of water.

3 Earwigs can be kept in a large jar or box with a mesh cover. They need a piece of turf and a layer of decaying leaves which should be kept damp (not wet). The earwigs will live quite happily in this for some time. It is not always realized that earwigs have wings and can fly, and they are unusual in that the female guards the eggs and newly hatched larvae.

4 Ants can be kept for a short time in a flat box or plastic seed tray with a piece of dark glass or perspex for a lid. The tray should be loosely filled with soil, leaving a gap at one corner where the ants can be fed with small quantities of jam or honey. They also need some protein, and will soon pick clean a small bone.

5 Following work from actual observation, plan specialized topics:
Useful insects – such as honey bee, silk moth, ladybird (eating aphids)
Beetles
Insects in the garden (park; woodland; field; on the seashore; in the town, etc.)
Pests – such as mosquito, aphid, locust, housefly, some caterpillars

Useful apparatus

Plastic sweet jars; other small jars; hand lenses; nylon mesh; rubber bands; acetate sheet; tin lids; collecting boxes

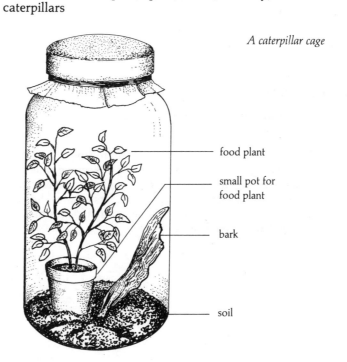

A caterpillar cage

food plant

small pot for food plant

bark

soil

19

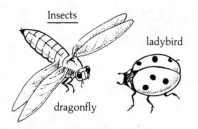

starfish

Echinoderms

Arthropods

Insects

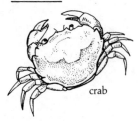

ladybird

dragonfly

Crustaceans

crab

Spiders

It is not always easy to convince children that, biologically, the word 'animal' applies to all the living things that are not plants. They naturally assume that only the mammals and reptiles are animals, and it is only by constant reference that they can be convinced that birds, fish and amphibians also fall into this group.

It is even more difficult to help them understand that such organisms as moths, snails, spiders, crabs, woodlice, whelks, sea anenomes and worms are also animals. They will have to see as many examples as possible.

Many of the familiar 'creepy-crawlies' that they already know are reasonably easy to collect, and studying them may help overcome the children's prejudices about some of the small animals. Why are they interested in a snail but repelled by a slug? Why do they want to tread on an earwig but pick up a ladybird? Why do they regard those fascinating animals, the spiders, as particularly repulsive?

A detailed study of one invertebrate is a good introduction to the whole group.

General notes

1 Invertebrate animals are found everywhere.
(See also sections 5 and 6).

2 Many invertebrate animals can be kept for the children to watch. See section 6 for suitable ways of keeping caterpillars and earwigs. Spiders are not difficult to keep provided they are fed properly. An ideal cage for spiders ensures that the webs are not broken when the animals are fed on small flies. They will also need drops of water.

3 Snails belong to the class of animals called the gastropods. They have a muscular foot and a coiled shell into which they can withdraw. Because of the spiral growth of the shell, it can grow longer as the snail matures, the direction of coiling always being the same for a given species. When looking at a snail, the children will also be able to see the two pairs of tentacles with the eye spots at the end of the longer pair, and the hole in the foot, near the edge of the shell, through which the snail breathes. If a snail is put on a piece of glass or perspex and viewed from beneath, the muscular movement of the foot can be seen, as well as the mouth opening. Snails secrete a sticky mucus which helps them move over any surface.

Snails are hermaphrodites, each snail being both male and female. When they mate, sperm is transferred from each snail to the other, and after mating, the snails lay eggs. The garden snail lays clutches of 20–30 eggs in damp soil. They are round, soft and semi-transparent, and usually hatch in about six weeks. Newly hatched small snails are like miniature adults, and they reach maturity in about one year. The garden snail feeds on vegetable matter and can be heard feeding because of its method of scraping leaves with its rasp-like tongue.

4 Earthworms – in spite of all the instructions found in many books for making wormeries, they are rarely successful. Children will learn much more by keeping them for a very short time in a bowl of soil and by watching them move.

Worms, like snails, are hermaphrodite, and they spend their lives underground. The familiar wormcasts are thrown up as the animal 'eats' its way through the soil. (They actually feed on the decaying vegetable matter found in soil). They cannot live in either completely dry or waterlogged ground.

5 There are other soil animals that can be looked at, such as slugs, woodlice and centipedes. Woodlice are easily found. They mostly eat decaying plants, and female woodlice carry their eggs between their hind legs until they hatch. The new, tiny woodlice can fend for themselves. Woodlice have a hard skin which does not grow, so they cast it, half at a time, to allow for growth.

Activities and experiments

1 The best way for children to learn about garden snails is to keep them. The children could make a suitable cage using a large wooden box, an aquarium or an old washing-up bowl, with a fine-mesh netting lid as shown in the illustration. Put a good layer of damp soil on the bottom of the container and arrange some stones so that the snails can get under or between them. Keep the cage in a fairly cool, shaded place and feed the snails daily with fresh green leaves. Remove any that are left uneaten or they will rot and become smelly. As snails do most of their feeding at night, see that they have fresh food in the evenings. If they are fed some rolled oats, droppings will be less messy and easier to remove from the cage. A little powdered chalk added to the oats provides the necessary calcium for shell formation. If the soil is kept moist, there is a good chance that the snails will lay eggs. The children can look for these and, once the young snails have hatched, can keep notes of their development.

   Note Snails hibernate in winter in sheltered cracks and crannies. They withdraw into their shells, sealing the opening with dried slime.

2 Further studies on snails can be done. How fast do they move? (See section 30). How far do snails move when outside? Shells can be marked with a dab of nail varnish and an attempt made to keep track of the marked snails. If snails are easy to find, make a study of shell spirals. Do shells spiral clockwise or anti-clockwise? Look at pond and sea snails as well as land snails.

3 Find out more about molluscs. This is a useful topic for schools with access to the shore and rock pools.

4 Make an invertebrate survey of a particular area.

Useful apparatus

Wood and plastic boxes; fine wire netting; tape measures; plastic bowls; hand lenses; red nail varnish; thick plastic or perspex sheet (useful for studying the movement of small animals as they walk on it); fishing nets

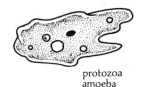

Single-celled animals

protozoa
amoeba

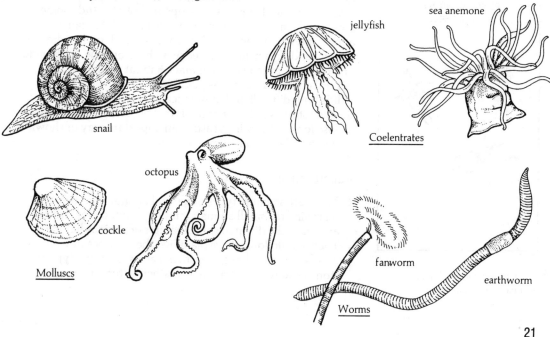

Multicellular animals

snail

jellyfish

sea anemone

Coelentrates

cockle

Molluscs

octopus

fanworm

earthworm

Worms

21

An animal or plant does not live in isolation. Each has its own particular habitat and each depends in some way or another on the other organisms within that habitat. To understand an organism fully, it is necessary to look at it in its environment.

Every small animal has to have food, protection and a suitable place to lay eggs or produce young. Because of their feeding habits, some may be classified as pests – cabbage white butterfly caterpillars eat cabbages and other brassicas; millipedes attack plant roots. In their hunt for food, some small animals can also be instrumental in pollinating flowers such as bees or some moths; ladybirds, for example, may kill greenfly which in turn, damage young plant shoots. All small animals are part of a food chain which further illustrates the interdependence of living things.

Children should be given the opportunity to study some of these small animals in the natural world, and this can be done almost anywhere – in a garden, on wasteland, in the school playground, in a field, at the edge of the shore line, at the side of a pond, or even in a home-made habitat that duplicates natural conditions as far as possible.

It is both difficult and impractical for children to make detailed studies of larger animals in their own environments, so a close look at the mini-beasts is an important way of showing them how plants and animals live together.

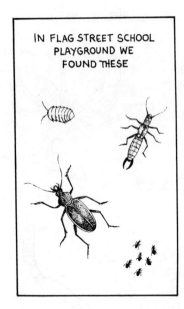

Card showing animals found in a particular habitat

General notes

1   There are so many types of natural habitat that, before searching for small animals, children should look around and learn the distinguishing features of various habitats. They should look at the plant life, the presence of water (pools, streams, bogs, marshland and seawater), type of soil, stones and rocks, particular weather features (prevailing winds), signs of habitation and signs of pollution. In this way they can build up a profile of the area.

2   The term used for the group of plants and animals found in any one habitat is a 'community'. Some examples of small communities are found in a stretch of hedge, a wall, a tree or a rock pool. Larger communities are found on moorland, in a pond, in a wood, on the shore or on a river bank. It is also possible to look at the natural community of a town.

3   Make any study reasonably detailed so that comparisons can be made, and plan records so that they can be used for future reference. While the children are doing all this, teach conservation. If a stone or log is moved, it should be replaced carefully.

4   It is worth finding out what part any of the small animals play in the food chains of the environment.

Green plants → → → snail → → → thrush → → → buzzard (See also section 4).

5   The animals that the children find will depend on the community studied, but could include:
   Insects (6 legs) – remember that the larvae will often differ considerably from the adult insect
   Spiders (8 legs)
   Centipedes and millipedes (many legs)
   Crustaceans (10–14 legs)
   Molluscs – snails and other shelled animals; slugs
   Worms
   Hollow-bodied animals – jelly fish and sea anenomes
   Here is also the opportunity to talk about the protozoa, single celled microscopic animals such as the amoeba. (Some classifications divide the animal kingdom into vertebrates, invertebrates and protozoa).

Activities and experiments

1 Study of a habitat – After selecting the habitat to be studied, make sure it is contained in some way. The length of a hedge should be marked out (e.g. a measured 3 m); the rock pool should be specified; the area of meadow or heathland should be clearly indicated; the town area should be marked on a plan.

The children need to understand that they must say exactly where they found each animal so that they can build up a picture of the area and the habits and needs of the animal (e.g. snail – hibernating in a crack in the dry stone wall; quite dry; 60 cm above ground).

2 Making a natural habitat –

a) A terrarium

Look at the diagram. An aquarium tank is needed, which can be an old one no longer completely watertight. Position it before putting in the contents because it will be too heavy to move when full. It should not be in direct sunlight.

Put a layer of soil on the bottom and cover this with about 6 cm of humus or peat. On this put some small stones, some dead wood or bark, some rotting leaves, a piece of tree branch with moss or lichen on it. Plant some small ferns, tufts of grass and some small plants such as groundsel, Spray it with water so that it is all damp, not wet, and cover the top with a sheet of glass or plastic. This should need little maintenance and, left alone, plants will grow and animals will appear. (They, or their eggs, will have been introduced with the leaves, bark and other items).

You should also put in a few woodlice or earwigs. Snails will eat the foliage too quickly and should be kept separately.

Children can vary this to create, say, a meadow or sand dune habitat.

b) An aquarium

A sea water aquarium is not easy to use unless you live where there is access to fresh sea water. This is probably best left to schools near the coast; others will have to make do with visits to the shore. (See also section 14).

Useful apparatus

Plastic bowls; trowels; plastic bags; aquarium tanks (all sizes); tape measures; string; camera; hand lenses

1. Earth & humus – bits of wood, bark etc.
2. Bark with insect larvae
3. Dead wood, pieces of tree stumps
4. Young fungi
5. Brambles with one layered naturally
6. Growing ivy
7. Grasses
8. Flowering plants

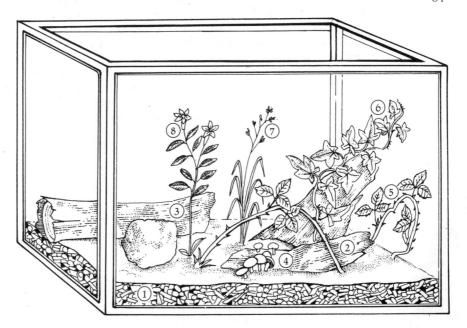

A terrarium for earwigs, woodlice, beetles etc.

Children are used to pet cats and dogs and, possibly, rabbits, guinea pigs and hamsters. They will also have been on visits to farms and zoos, or have seen other mammals on film or on television. Many are used to having pets at home or at school, but a pet should mean more than an animal in which they are interested for a short time and which, after a while, becomes a chore instead of a pleasure.

Even the youngest children can be taught to look after small animals, to take an interest in their welfare and to learn something about their lives and habits. Children will need to be helped with this, but they should be given definite, even if minimal, responsibility for some part of the animal's care. Supervision is always essential, but this should be as unobtrusive as possible so that the child feels in charge of the animal.

It is by watching an animal – in this case a small mammal – that children can learn the characteristics of these animals and will also, it is hoped, realize that keeping pets must be taken seriously. A cuddly kitten grows into a cat which may live 12 years or more, and the rabbit which was fun to play with in the summer has to be fed and have its cage cleaned out on a cold January morning.

Note　Keeping animals in school so that the children can watch them is an excellent idea, provided that they can be adequately cared for over the weekend and during the school holidays. If this is not possible, then keep borrowed animals for a few days only.

General notes

1 All mammals have features in common. They are warm-blooded, have an internal skeleton and four limbs, are more or less covered with fur or hair and many of them have tails. With very few exceptions, mammals do not lay eggs. The young develop inside the body of the female and are usually born in a fairly developed state. Those born in nests (rabbits, cats, mice, etc.) are helpless at birth and need to be cared for by the parents. Those born in the open (deer, cows, horses, etc.) are able to run soon after birth but are still fed by the female. All mammals are fed on milk produced by the mammary glands of the female. Mammals vary considerably in size, shape, colour, feeding and habitat.

2 Pets which can be kept in school are fairly limited. They need to be housed in reasonably small cages and to be easy to feed. If children are going to handle them (and they must be taught to do this properly) the pets must not bite or scratch.

Rabbits – the size of rabbits varies, but the black and white Dutch rabbits tend to stay small. The hutch must be sufficiently large for the rabbit to move freely and to sit up without the ears touching the roof. They tame easily and do not smell if the cage is cleaned out regularly. If a pair is kept, the female will produce a new litter every few weeks. The babies must not be disturbed until they are two or three weeks old (the female will probably destroy them if they are touched when newly born). Rabbits can be handled if done so carefully, and do not seem to mind being weighed and measured. Once used to the children, they will be undisturbed by noise and movement around them.

Guinea pigs – these animals make ideal pets. They are small, easily handled, easy to feed and do not breed too quickly. The gestation period is about 10 weeks, and the young can be touched and looked at when only a few hours old. They are miniatures of the adults when born, and are covered with fur and have their eyes open. They will nibble green food and run about when less than a day old. They are nervous little animals and rarely become as tame as rabbits, but children find them very attractive.

Mice – mice can be kept indoors in small cages but they

tend to smell however clean they are kept. They can be weighed, measured and handled and are very cheap to feed. Two females will live together quite happily, but two males tend to fight.

Hamsters – these are pretty little animals, fascinating to watch as they pouch their food and sit up on their hind legs, but they are basically nocturnal and are not very active by day. They will often bite if handled, but they are easy to keep. If the children are not allowed to pick them up, they make good classroom pets. They need a strong cage as they will chew through thin wood very quickly.

Gerbils – these little animals are very active and this makes them particularly attractive. Like hamsters, they will soon chew through a wooden cage, and will often bite if handled, but they do not smell and are easy to feed. They will chew up everything chewable and will make untidy nests from paper, material, etc.

3 All these animals can be fed on oats, cornflakes, hard baked bread and fresh food such as carrots, apples, nuts, dandelion leaves, fresh grass. They all need water.

Activities and experiments

1 Looking at the animals – children can measure (length from tip of nose to base of tail) and weigh the animal. Mice can be put into a paper bag (paper only) for a few moments for weighing. They can also note colouring, shape and size of ears and eyes, type of limbs and claws and how the animal moves. If the animals are kept in school, or can be seen at regular intervals, speed of growth can be measured, and the length of time between birth and full growth recorded.

2 If the animal is kept in school, caring for it is part of the study. Children will need to know the sort of food required

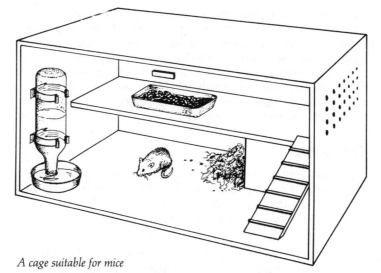

A cage suitable for mice

and the quantity to give. They will also realize that the animal needs regular cleaning because of the amount of urine and solid waste that is excreted.

3 Problem solving – while studying any particular animal, the children can try to find the answers to various problems.
  A rabbit will eat half its own weight in food a day. Do you do this?
  Are a cat's whiskers any use to it?
  How far can a mouse move in half a minute?
  How much food does a guinea pig eat in a week?
  Does a baby animal grow proportionately in weight and length?
  Do animals feeding on different foods have different teeth? (Compare the teeth of a cat, a carnivore, with those of a rabbit, a vegetarian).

Useful apparatus

Animal cages; animal observation cage; balance; scales; tape measures; paper bags; feeding bowls; plastic buckets, small shovels

Children who have been made aware of the wide variety of living things, and who have begun to classify them into groups of some sort, need to know something more about the examples they see. Some of the characteristics of each individual organism can be shown by asking them to look at shape and size. This necessarily involves some mathematics, but it is always a good idea to integrate subjects and to accept that there is an inevitable overlap.

General notes

1 Animals grow to a definite size and shape and cease growing appreciably once full size is reached. Plants continue to grow throughout their lives, and have a less definite size and shape. Trees add to their girth annually, and the rings formed can be used to find out the age of a felled tree.

2 The largest animal on earth, and the largest animal that has ever lived, is the blue whale. It can weigh up to 120 tonnes – 40 times heavier than the largest elephant. It is a great deal larger than any of the prehistoric giant dinosaurs.

   The largest plants are trees and the largest in the world is the Californian redwood, which can grow to a height of more than 112 m, and live to an age of over 3000 years.

3 Some plants and animals are so small that they can only be seen with a microscope, but some tiny plants that are more familiar can be spotted. (For example, the duckweed that grows on the top of ponds has leaves which are about 5 mm across.) One of the things that children can do is to find out for themselves facts about weight and measurements of many plants and animals. Children like doing this, and will quite readily accept that an elephant has to be drawn smaller than life size, but an ant has to be drawn larger.

4 The largest animals live in the sea because of the support given by the water. This means that they do not have to have a skeleton strong enough to support their weight, as land animals do. A whale will die on land not because it cannot breathe air, but because its skeleton cannot support its great weight.

5 The shape of a plant or animal depends on its habitat and conditions of life. Here are some examples:
   The streamlined shape of most fish assists them to move through water.
   The frog has jointed limbs for moving on land and webbed feet for swimming.
   The giraffe is adapted for feeding from foliage high up in trees.
   The mole is shaped for burrowing and has powerful front limbs for digging.
   Climbing plants do not need strong woody stems for support.
   Water plants are shaped so that they float in or on water.

6 Limbs of animals have to support the body weight, and the area of the foot needs to be broad enough to prevent the animal sinking into the ground. (Look at the feet of a camel.)
   A cow weighs about 400 kg, so each leg has to support 100 kg when it is standing. As the animal moves, the weight on each leg is increased and so the limbs must be sufficiently strong to carry this extra weight. (See also section 13.)

7 Heat is lost from the surface of living organisms. Warm-blooded animals generate heat within their bodies and maintain a constant body temperature. These animals must lose excess heat in warm conditions and retain it in cold. Cold-blooded animals absorb heat from their

Plants tend to grow throughout their lives

Animals grow to a definite size

surroundings, and tend to become sluggish or hibernate in cold weather.

An elephant has a small body area in relation to its weight. Its large ears and folded skin increase body surface, giving greater heat loss which is necessary in the hot climate of its habitat.

A polar bear is a large animal, thus producing a great deal of body heat to withstand the cold. This is retained by thick hair that covers even the soles of its feet.

8 Plants absorb light energy to enable them to manufacture food. Leaves often have a large surface to give them maximum exposure.

9 Measurements most commonly used when studying living things are:
a) Length – of animals (from tip of nose to end of tail)
b) Height – of plants or standing animals (the height of a horse is measured from ground to shoulder)
c) Girth – of tree trunks, limbs of animals
d) Weight
e) Wing span – of birds, insects, bats
f) Volume – of water animals
g) Surface area – of leaves, whole animal

Activities and experiments

1 Find the answers to set questions such as:
What is the largest land animal? Where does it live? What does it weigh?
What is the smallest mammal in Britain/Europe/Asia/the world?
Which is the largest animal that has ever lived?
Which tree that you have seen has leaves with the largest area?

2 Find the average hand length of adult males and females, and of, say, boys and girls of specific ages (5, 7, 9 or 11 years). Measure from the bottom of the thumb joint (where it meets the wrist) to the top of the longest finger. Measure 50 in each group if possible. What conclusions can the children draw from these results?

3 Study the shape and size of any animal in detail, using charts which can be adapted for use with plants, insects, fish etc.

4 Devise experiments to find out if an animal with a large surface area is also heavy. Does surface area increase directly with weight?

5 Compare speed of growth and life span.
For growing speed, find out the length of time from birth till full growth
Does a large animal necessarily live longer than a small one?
It may be easier to look at some of the smaller animals for this – frog, newt, butterfly, housefly, ladybird, snail

6 Experiment with the speed of growth in plants. Find out how long it takes from planting until a plant produces seeds (use beans, any annuals, willow-herb, shepherd's purse, etc.)

Useful apparatus

Balances; personal scales (an animal such as a dog or cat can be weighed by holding it while standing on scales and subtract your weight from the total weight); tape measures; modelling clay; squared paper; Guiness Book of Records

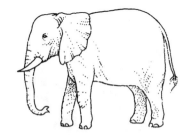

The large and the small. If the flea was drawn to the same scale as the elephant, it would be impossible to see.

bulbs and corms

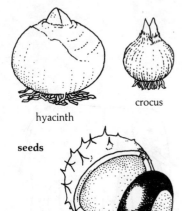

hyacinth

crocus

seeds

horse chestnut

Reproduction in plants can be from seeds or can be vegetative

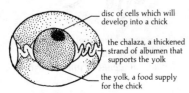

disc of cells which will develop into a chick

the chalaza, a thickened strand of albumen that supports the yolk

the yolk, a food supply for the chick

A cross-sectional view through a fertilized hen's egg

One of the characteristics of living organisms is their ability to reproduce. Without this, there would be no continuity of life, and even the youngest children readily appreciate that plants and animals are capable of producing new offspring. They will also understand that, although such things as cars and aeroplanes can move freely and need fuel to keep them running, they are not able to reproduce themselves and so cannot be alive.

General notes

1 Living organisms produce offspring that are more or less like the parents, although they can be completely dissimilar in the early stages. For example:

Tadpole → → → Frog
Caterpillar → → → Moth or butterfly
  The seedlings of many plants are often difficult to identify.

2 Sexual reproduction involves the union of male and female cells. Most living organisms reproduce sexually. Seeds are the product of sexual reproduction in plants.

3 Most animals reproduce themselves by producing eggs which are fertilized and develop into young animals. Fertilization is the fusion of the female cells (the ova) and the male cells (the sperm). In mammals, fertilization occurs within the female's body where the embryo develops, the period of gestation differing from animal to animal. Other animals lay eggs, inside which the young develop after the eggs are laid. In some animals fertilization is external, the male shedding sperm over the eggs after the female has laid them (amphibians and most fishes). Animals that are born in nests tend to be less developed than those born in the open. The latter need to be able to move away from predators from the moment of birth.

4 Plants usually produce seeds in large numbers to ensure that each species will continue. Flowers are pollinated (the pollen carries the male cells) in various ways – by wind, by insects, by self-pollination – and once the seeds are formed, the flowers wither and die. A seed develops and grows into a mature plant resembling the parent plant. The tiny seeds of a poppy will grow into new poppy plants and acorns will grow into oak trees.

5 Asexual reproduction does not involve two individuals. In its simplest form, the organisms divide into two (e.g. amoeba). Many plants can reproduce vegetatively (bulbs, corms, tubers, runners, budding, cuttings and grafting). Mosses, fungi and ferns reproduce from spores.

6 Asexual reproduction produces identical offspring – very useful for the gardener – but the offspring resulting from sexual reproduction can be significantly different, although obviously belonging to the same species. For example, cats can be black, white, tabby, etc. and a mother cat may produce a batch of kittens which are all different colours. In this way new features and characteristics develop and new species may eventually appear.

These, and many other animals, lay eggs

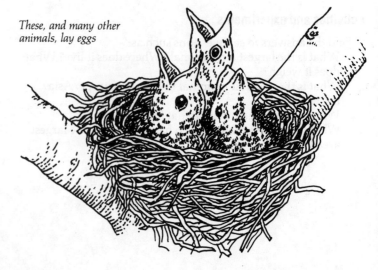

Activities and experiments

1 The best way of watching the process of reproduction is to keep animals. Guinea pigs are ideal small mammals. Their gestation period is about 10 weeks and their young are so well developed at birth that they can be carefully handled almost immediately. Mice are also easy to keep and are more active by day than hamsters.

2 Other suitable animals are land and water snails, insects (larvae to adult) and frogs (spawn to young frog).

3 Pets with new offspring – a cat with kittens, a dog with puppies – can be brought to school for a short time so that the children can compare the young animals with the adults. After they have seen these familiar animals, they can find out more about other animals and record the following details:
a) Name
b) Gestation period (e.g. cat, 63 days; cow, 282 days; horse, 340 days)
c) Number of young normally born
d) Development of young at birth
e) Amount of parental care
f) Age when animal is capable of fending for itself
g) Age of maturity
h) Life span

4 Look at a hen's egg as an example of a bird's egg. Even though the chances are that this will be unfertilized, the children can see the general structure of an egg.
a) How is the growing baby bird protected?
b) On what does the unhatched bird feed?
c) How does a baby bird break through the shell and hatch out of the egg?
    Find out about the eggs of other animals (e.g., reptiles, amphibians, fish, snails and insects). How are these protected? Do egg-laying parents look after their offspring? How long does the embryo take to develop before hatching?
    The children can find out as much as possible about eggs and write up their findings.

5 Further developments:
a) Sexual reproduction of plants
b) Animal families – looking at the family as a unit
c) Family trees and heredity
d) Development of the human baby
e) Growing plants without seeds

Useful apparatus

Cages for small animals; pictures of animals and their young; plant pots and potting compost; bags for seed collections

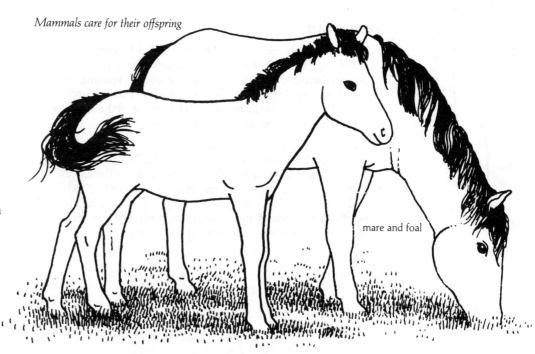

Mammals care for their offspring

mare and foal

29

Children know what they look like. They know that they have two arms, two legs, two ears, two eyes and a nose. They know that they can move from place to place using their legs, and that if they scratch themselves they will bleed, but will heal reasonably rapidly. They will also realize that they have to eat and drink, and connect this vaguely with growing and staying alive. Some might mention that they need food for 'energy', with little understanding as to what this means. They are also interested in their own bodies, but often know very little about them. Very few appreciate that they belong to that group of animals known as mammals – and that they have, therefore, something in common with cows, mice and hedgehogs!

Any project undertaken should include looking at living things in general, and themselves in particular, so that they will begin to understand something of their own anatomy and physiology, and the need to care for their own bodies.

General notes

1 Humans are mammals and therefore warm-blooded and vertebrate, but unlike other mammals in that they have assumed an erect position for moving about. The human skeleton is made up of 206 bones of different shapes and sizes. The largest is the femur (thigh bone) and the smallest are the three tiny bones in the ear (the ossicles).

2 Like other living things, mammals reproduce, feed, breathe, grow, move, excrete and react to stimuli. Growth is very fast between birth and six months old, and again in the early teens. The head stops growing before the rest of the body, and is virtually full size by the age of 10. Once full height is reached (between 18 and 20 years) a person will not grow any taller, but may grow fatter and heavier.

3 The surface of the body is covered with skin. This skin helps to regulate temperature and protects the body from water, harmful substances and bacteria. The colour of the skin depends on the pigment in it, and skin colour among humans varies very considerably.

4 Any study of ourselves can include basic health education – care of skin, nails, hair, feet, teeth, eyes and ears, clothing, food and exercise. Also homes and families.

Activities and experiments

1 Taking a look at ourselves
a) Get children to take a general look at themselves and each other. What are the things they all have in common? They all breathe, move, feed, grow; they can see, hear and feel things; they have to get rid of waste materials.
b) What shape are humans? Even the youngest infants can draw the approximate shape of the human body, showing arms, legs, head and trunk.
c) Basically all humans are the same shape, but discuss differences between boys and girls (men and women); between tall and short; between fat and thin, etc.
d) Look at the colour of skin, hair and eyes. Talk about the differences.
e) As skin covers the whole of our bodies, its importance is obvious. Find out its functions, and find out how it should be cared for.
f) Find out about respiration and breathing. The rate of respiration can be measured by watching the chest movements (very easy if watching a sleeping baby). Rate of respiration and heartbeat (pulse) can be compared.

2 Follow this up with some work on bones and movement (see section 13).

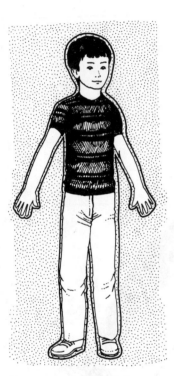

The approximate area of skin covering the body is the outline $\times 2$

3 Take measurements of children in the class, and find out such things as average height and weight for boys and girls of a given age.

Draw round feet and find the length (or width). Have the tallest children got the biggest feet?

Estimate the area of skin covering the body. This can only be an approximation but will show how extensive it is. Draw round a child lying on a sheet of paper. Cut out this outline, and then cut another the same size. This will give some idea.

4 Look at eyes and ears
Devise experiments to find out how far away we can see or hear things.

Find out how eyes and ears are used for communication and for making decisions. (This can play a part in safety. For example – is that plank wide enough to talk on? I can't see any traffic but I can hear something).

Discuss the position of the eyes and ears both in humans and other animals. Is this important?

5 Look at the other senses
Investigate smell and taste. (If devising tasting experiments, stress that children must only taste the things you say they may.)

By experimenting, show how important the sense of touch is. Let children find out if they can distinguish hot from cold, smooth from rough, etc. Can they recognize objects by feel only?

Discuss pain and how essential it is to make us feel something sharp or hot on our hand, for example. Pain, such as toothache, also indicates that there is something wrong.

6 Work on food can vary according to age, but it should include information about the types of foods needed and the amounts that should be eaten. This can include something about digestion of food and the necessity of getting rid of waste.

7 Other topics:
a) Hair and eye colouring
b) The work of the heart and the blood
c) Personal growth charts (taking measurements each term) showing height, weight, arm and leg length, hand span, circumference of head, neck, chest, waist and thigh, foot length
d) Respiration and breathing
e) Temperature – keeping warm or cool

Useful apparatus

Height measure; personal scales; tape measures; string; squared paper; minute timers; tape recorder; model skeleton; mirror

A great deal of variation – but all humans

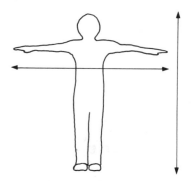

It is said that a person's height is the same as the measurement between the fingertips with the arms stretched out sideways. Is this true?

Children seem to be fascinated by bones and skeletons, probably because they are synonymous with creepy stories. This fascination can be used to get them interested in the general structure and movement of vertebrates. Many children seem to think that only humans have skeletons, and it is only when they are prompted that they realize that cats, dogs, horses, fish, frogs and tortoises have skeletons too. In fact all the mammals, birds, fish, reptiles and amphibians from the tiniest bird to the massive blue whale, are vertebrate and so have a bony framework.

Some other animals – insects, crabs, lobsters etc. – have a hard outer covering called an exo-skeleton.

General notes

1 The skeleton is the bony framework supporting and protecting the softer parts of the body. The muscles attached to it enable the body to move. Movable connections between bones are called joints. The skull protects the brain and the rib cage protects the heart and lungs.

Most vertebrate skeletons are made of bone, a hard substance composed mainly of calcium compounds. Many bones are tubes, so they are light but comparatively strong. The soft inner tissue (the marrow) manufactures red blood cells. The ends of some bones are covered with a softer substance (cartilage) which eases movement. The skeletons of sharks and some other related fish (e.g. skate and dogfish) are composed of cartilage.

2 The human skeleton consists of 206 bones ranging from the tiny ear bones to the large femur or thigh bone. The backbone (vertebral column and spine) is made up of 33 bones called vertebrae. The skull is made up of several bones fused together, of which only the lower jaw is movable. The 12 pairs of ribs, together with the sternum or

breast bone and the chest vertebra, make a bony cage which protects the heart and lungs. The collar bones (clavicles) and shoulder blades (scapulae) support the arms and provide muscle attachment. The pelvis, a ring of strong bones, partly encloses the lower abdominal organs. The thigh bones are attached to the pelvis.

3 Some bones, such as those in the skull, are joined together but there is no movement between them, while others are connected loosely so that movement is possible. Bones meeting at a movable joint are covered with cartilage at the point of contact and connected by ligaments. The amount of movement varies according to the type of joint.

4 All movements of the body are produced by muscles, which is why much of the body tissue is muscular. Muscles vary in size from the tiny muscles moving the eye to the large thigh muscles. Some muscles can be moved at will (the arm or leg, turning the head, bending the back). Others work automatically (those in the intestine). The heart is a strong, muscular pump that beats continually.

5 Although all mammals have basically the same skeletal structure, there are many adaptations, and children can find many examples for themselves.

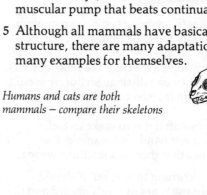

Humans and cats are both mammals – compare their skeletons

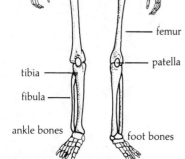

skull

lower jaw

clavicle

sternum

humerus

vertebra

radius

ulna

pelvis

femur

patella

tibia

fibula

ankle bones

foot bones

Activities and experiments

1 Bones are not difficult to collect. They are frequently found on beaches, moors, in parks and in gardens. It may be difficult to identify the animal to which they belong, but it is usually possible to name the type of bone. Chicken and rabbit bones from the kitchen can be boiled in detergent and then dried in the oven. A large bone, obtained from the butcher, can be cut across to show the strong outer bone and the hollow centre.

2 Bones have to be strong enough to support the animal, but light enough to allow it to move about. The strength of tubes – which is the shape of long limb bones – can be tested by experiment. Rolled tubes made from three pieces of ordinary paper (A5 size) can be used to support a dish of water. Can the children make tubes strong enough to support their own weight?

3 Look at joints – this is intended to show children how joints move. By observation and experiment, they can find out which move freely (shoulder, hip), which move in one direction only (knee, elbow), and which allow turning and twisting movements (neck, arm when turning the hand). They can decide what would happen if the knee and elbow joints moved in both directions. Look at finger joints and look at all the things that can be done with the hands. What would happen if the fingers could not move freely? Cover the hands with stiff paper 'mittens' and see how this limits activity. Try walking up steps without bending the knees at all.

4 With a partner, children can try to identify the position of the main bones in their own bodies.

5 A visit to the zoo or natural history museum can be used to learn more about other animals:
   Many mammals have tails, which are extensions of the backbone. Are these of any use?
   A giraffe has a very long neck. Are there a lot of bones in it? (It has got only the same number of neck vertebrae as humans.)
   Have snakes got bones?

6 Look at skulls in a museum or in pictures and see the variation in teeth. Try to find out how teeth vary according to the food eaten.

7 Find out more about the bones of fish and birds. Look at the exo-skeletons of crabs and lobsters. Do these outer shells grow as bones do?

Useful apparatus

Tape measures; balances; boxes for collections; cling film; hand lenses; model skeleton; collections of bones; stiff paper; tie-on labels

How many joints can be found in the hand?
Look at hand movements

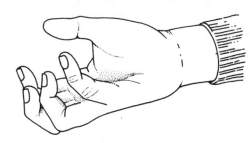

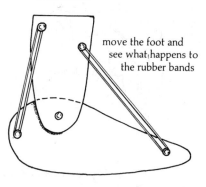

rubber bands behave like muscles

move the foot and see what happens to the rubber bands

Cut out the two shapes shown in the drawing

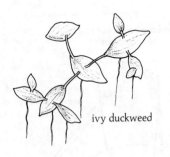

lesser duckweed

ivy duckweed

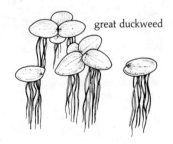

great duckweed

Water weeds

The first plants and animals that appeared on the earth lived in water. Of the millions of living organisms now in existence, a great many spend their whole lives in water, some in the sea and some in fresh water. Although some schools do not have easy access to the sea and seashore, it is reasonably easy to find freshwater habitats – ponds, lakes, streams, rivers, ditches, canals, ornamental pools and even garden rainwater butts.

It may not always be possible for children to make a study of pond life, but it is important that they are given the opportunity to see how organisms have adapted to living in water. Even if it is necessary to take the 'pond' to them, it is well worth doing, and it is not difficult to set up some sort of aquarium in which specimens can be kept for a short time. Obviously, this is not as good as a visit to a pond or stream, but teachers working in the middle of towns may find such a visit is impractical.

General notes

1 Some flowering plants grow completely submerged and these show the greatest adaptation. They are fully supported by the water. All parts of these plants absorb water and the gases dissolved in it, and there are no stomata ('breathing' pores). Some plants are rooted in shallow water, and have floating leaves. Others are completely free-floating. Both these types of water plants have stomata on the upper surfaces of their leaves through which air can enter.

Examples of flowering water plants include:
a) Totally submerged plants – Canadian pondweed (Elodea), water milfoil
b) Rooted plants with floating leaves – water lilies
c) Free-floating plants – duckweeds, frogbit
   Most water plants are perennials and are adapted to survive cold conditions. During the winter, some sink to the bottom of the pond where the water is warmer. The tops of some die back and new shoots appear next spring from the rhizomes buried in the mud. Others form 'winter buds' which sink into the mud when the parent plant dies, and these give rise to new plants the following year.

2 Most algae are found in water, the majority of species growing in the sea (seaweeds are algae). The largest group of freshwater algae is made up of green algae. Some of these are single-celled, while others are made up of groups of cells forming filaments. Examples of freshwater algae are:
a) Single-cell algae – Diatoms (some are free-floating, others are attached to stones). A microscope is needed to see these attractive, tiny plants.
b) Filamentous algae – Spirogyra (found in floating masses in ponds).

3 Water animals – while looking at life in a pond, children could be introduced to the use of a microscope. Even very young children can use a simple binocular microscope. They may be able to look at water fleas and shrimps, water snail eggs, larvae of mosquitoes, paramecium, etc. Other animals to look at in fresh water include: worms and leeches, snails and other molluscs, water shrimps, insect larva, frogs and newts (and their tadpoles), fish.

4 All fish live in water, absorbing oxygen through their gills. (As water flows over the gills, oxygen passes into the blood stream.)

5 Some animals spend only part of their life cycle in water.

Mosquito Larvae → → → pupae → → → adult flying
(in water)   (in water)   insect

Dragonfly nymph → → → adult flying insect
(in water for up
to two years)

Tadpole → → → frog or newt
(in water)   (on land and in water)

Activities and experiments

1 Visit to a pond, stream or rock pool (see also section 41) –
Prepare the children for the visit so that they have some idea
as to what to look for, and teach them the basic rules of
conservation. (Do no damage; move stones and anything
else carefully; return all animals to where they belong after
they have been looked at.) Look for:
a) Environment of pond – position, size, depth, plant life
around, other features
b) Plants (submerged or floating)
c) Free swimming animals (on the surface or in the water)
d) Animals attached to plants, stones or rock

2 Making a fresh water habitat – It is possible to build a pond
outside by digging a hole and lining it with thick plastic
sheeting, but it is probably more practical to use small
aquaria indoors (see diagram). If proper tanks are not
available, use washing up bowls. These can be used to house
small fish, snails, tadpoles, etc. It is not always possible to
catch fish but one or two small goldfish can be kept to show
how fish move, feed, etc. Water snails kept in the tank with
them will help to keep the sides free of algae.

3 Further developments:
a) Streamlining and shape (fishes)
b) Water pollution
c) Life of the salmon
d) Living in the sea

Useful apparatus

Small aquaria; plastic bowls; fishing nets; kitchen sieves; small
buckets; microscope; hand lenses; washed sand

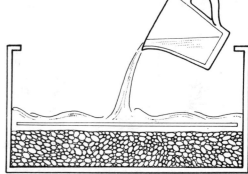

*A small aquarium for tadpoles, snails or small fish (two
little goldfish). Light should enter it from one side only*

To avoid disturbing the soil, cover it
with a stiff sheet of paper before
filling with water

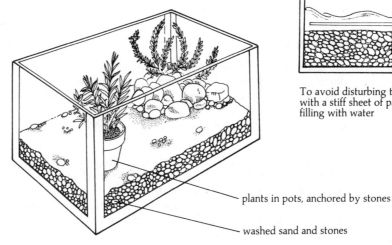

plants in pots, anchored by stones

washed sand and stones

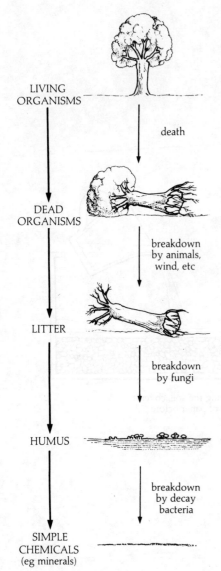

LIVING
ORGANISMS

death

DEAD
ORGANISMS

breakdown
by animals,
wind, etc

LITTER

breakdown
by fungi

HUMUS

breakdown
by decay
bacteria

SIMPLE
CHEMICALS
(eg minerals)

Most children have at some time found a 'fairy ring' of toadstools in the grass but have not associated them with other common fungi such as mushrooms, which can be eaten, and the large bracket fungi seen on dead and dying trees.

Another group of common but unusual fungi are the moulds. The fungi differ from other plants because they are not green, and so cannot manufacture their own food. (The green chlorophyll is needed to absorb light energy for building up of plants foods from simple materials.) Because of this, all fungi have to obtain ready-made food from the substances on which they grow.

They are also seedless, reproducing themselves by means of spores. These are so tiny and dust-like that they are always around, floating in the air, and then developing if they settle on a suitable growing medium. This makes moulds very easy to grow. They are an ideal study when the temperature and weather prevent outdoor activities.

General notes

1 Moulds are very simple fungi which will grow on almost any damp organic matter. Like all fungi, they produce a mass of branched threads which penetrate the food material and send out digestive juices. These dissolve the food so that the mould can absorb it. Because light is not needed for food manufacture, moulds can grow in darkness.

2 Moulds and other fungi are important decomposers. If dead plant and animal material did not decay, the earth's surface would be covered with a mass of dead remains (and life could not exist). Decay bacteria and fungi break down these remains, releasing chemical materials which can be used for new growth.

3 The appearance of moulds on the surface of bread, animal droppings and fruit is fluffy and often blue, white or green. At the end of some of the surface threads, swellings containing spores will form. When they are ripe, these swollen heads burst and release a mass of spores into the air.

4 Toadstools and other fungi are more complicated than moulds but they still consist of a mass of threads growing into the food material. At certain times of the year, and often in autumn, the threads form large swellings which grow into the familiar fungi seen on trees, on the ground and on decaying wood. Many are mushroom shaped but others can look like orange peel, fans or the familiar 'puff-balls'.

5 Some fungi are edible but some are very poisonous. It needs to be stressed that no fungi should be eaten unless it is absolutely certain that they are harmless.

6 Not all fungi live on dead material. A few attack living things and can cause serious plant diseases. (The Irish famine of the 19th century was caused by a fungus attacking the potato crops.) Athlete's Foot is a fungal disease.

7 Yeasts are very unusual fungi. They consist of separate, spherical cells which reproduce very rapidly under the right conditions. They feed on sugars found in plants and, as they digest these, form carbon dioxide and alcohol. They are, therefore, of commercial importance in brewing beer and making wine, and in baking (the released carbon dioxide makes the dough rise).

Activities and experiments

1 Growing moulds – put a thick slice of bread into a plastic box, damp it with water and put on the lid. Leave the box in a warm place. At the end of a week, look at the bread and see if mould has grown on it. If the progress of growth is to be watched, cover the box with cling film instead of a lid. Examine any moulds that have grown with a hand lens or microscope. One mould likely to appear is mucor (sometimes called pin-head mould because the ripe spore-filled heads stick up like pins). Try growing moulds on other materials.

2 Look for moulds on decaying vegetable matter, on foods, on damp walls and on growing plants. Mould on cheese is often not wanted but some cheeses have particular moulds introduced as part of their make up. Stilton and Danish Blue are examples.

3 Go out on an autumn hunt for fungi. Specimens can be drawn, photographed or carefully collected (remembering that some are poisonous). Note where each type was found so that areas can be compared. Many fungi do not have simple names, so identification is extremely difficult.

4 The spores of mushrooms and toadstools are formed on the gills under the umbrella shaped top. Find a fully open, ripe cap and leave it, gills down, on a piece of paper for several hours. There will then be a spore print on the paper.

5 Yeast – use either fresh baker's yeast or dried yeast. Put about one teaspoonful of sugar in some warm water (*not* hot). Stir well and leave for one or two hours in a warm place. The yeast will froth up as it multiplies and breaks down the sugar, releasing carbon dioxide. Using yeast, bread can be made from any standard recipe, or wine can be brewed from a commercial wine kit.

6 Certain moulds, notably penicillium, have become very important because the drug extracted from them is used in fighting bacterial infections. Find out the story of the discovery of penicillin.

Useful apparatus

Plastic boxes; cling film; plastic bags for collecting; small dishes; hand lenses; microscope

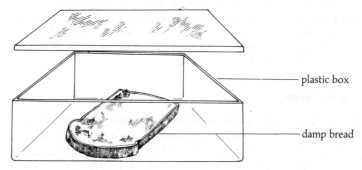

Growing moulds. Put the lid on the box and leave in a warm place

plastic box

damp bread

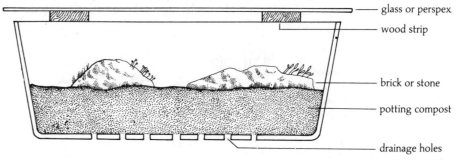

A moss jungle in a plastic box. Introduce mossy stones and keep damp

glass or perspex

wood strip

brick or stone

potting compost

drainage holes

37

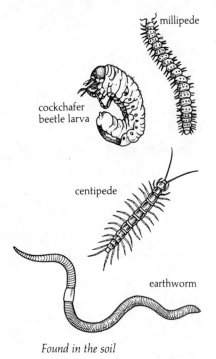

millipede

cockchafer
beetle larva

centipede

earthworm

Found in the soil

If children have been planting seeds or making gardens, they have almost certainly been using soil. The town child's attitude towards it can be seen by indiscriminate use of the word 'dirt' instead of the word 'soil', and even the older child, used to seeing planting, growing and harvesting, often does not realize how much soils can vary.

Most young children take great pleasure in digging and playing about with soil. While they have been digging holes, they may have noticed roots, worms and pieces of decaying leaves, and may have found that there are stones which sink to the bottom when they make mud.

They may have the opportunity to see earth-moving machinery at work, and to see how the layers vary from the top vegetation to the lower, sandy areas. However children are introduced to this particular topic, they should in the end have some idea of the importance of soil as a growing medium for plants, and how its fertility affects us all.

General notes

1 Soil consists of humus (decayed plant and animal material) and particles of rock broken down by the action of water, heat and plant growth. Top soil is generally darker because of the humus in it – sub-soil contains very little. Soil also contains sand, clay, stones, mineral salts, bacteria, water and air. It provides the growing medium for plants – air, water, food materials, anchorage and protection for seeds and roots.

woodlouse

Found on the surface, under leaves and stones

earwig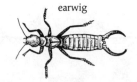

2 Soils vary considerably. Sandy soils are warm, loose, full of air spaces and easily worked. They are well drained but do not retain sufficient water during dry spells.

Clay soils are cold, heavy to work, and contain few air spaces. Because the particles are packed close together, they become waterlogged. They contain more mineral salts than sandy soils.

Loam is a mixture of clay, sand and humus.

Chalky soils are greyish in colour, and have a characteristic plant growth because only certain plants can tolerate the excessive amount of lime in chalk soil.

3 Soil constantly flooded by the sea contains too much salt (sodium chloride) for most plants. Plants growing in salt marsh areas cannot absorb water in this concentrated solution of salt, so they only take in water during times of heavy rain, and are capable of storing this fresh water within themselves.

4 There are many living organisms to be found in soil:
   Bacteria, protozoa, moulds and other fungi
   Eelworms, mites, millipedes, centipedes, insect larvae
   Earthworms, ants, slugs, beetles

Some feed on decaying materials, some on living roots and some prey on each other.

5 Other animals are associated with soil in some way. Moles live in underground burrows, feeding mainly on earthworms; rabbits and foxes make burrows where their young are born; the larvae of all hawk moths pupate in soil; snail eggs are laid in soil.

6 Soil provides anchorage for growing plants as well as the water and mineral salts necessary for building up their food.

Activities and experiments

1 Examine a large bowlful of soil. Spread it out on a polythene sheet and find out what is in it. What type of soil is it? (Sandy, clay, full of humus, etc.) Shake up a small quantity in a jar of water and leave it to settle. Look at the constituents.

2 Collect soil samples in jars from different areas and label them. Compare.

3 If children have access to a garden, they can dig and make a soil profile.

4 Put different samples of soils in small flower pots. Sprinkle mustard seeds on top. Water them all regularly, giving each the same amount of water, and keep them all in the same place. Watch the growth. Is this affected by the type of soil?

5 Get children to devise their own experiments to answer the following:
   Which type of soil drains the best? Which retains too much water?
   Which dries out the quickest?
   Which supports the most animal life?
   With a particular sample of soil, how many stones, whole leaves, pieces of plant root, etc. were found in it?

Useful apparatus

Margarine pots with lids; plastic bowls; plastic bags; polythene sheeting; trowels and spoons; mayonnaise jars (or other tall jars for soil samples); hand lenses; mustard seeds (or other seeds); small flower pots

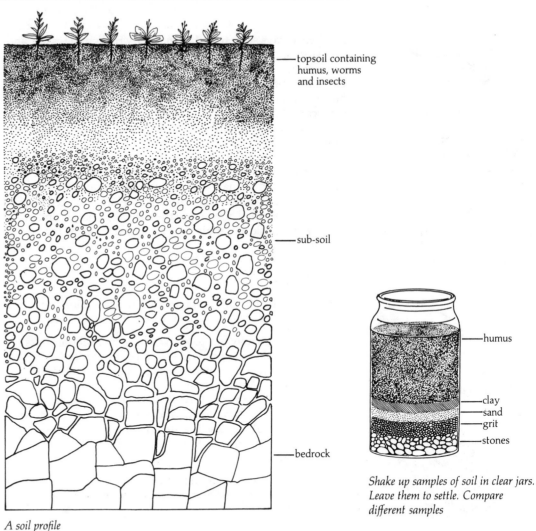

topsoil containing humus, worms and insects

sub-soil

bedrock

A soil profile

humus

clay
sand
grit
stones

Shake up samples of soil in clear jars. Leave them to settle. Compare different samples

rocks cut to shape

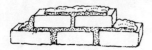

mortar

clay tiles   clay bricks

concrete   cement

Building materials

Children always seem to be fascinated by rocks and fossils, and since stones, rocks and soils can be found in almost any environment, they make interesting starters for a worthwhile scientific topic. Geological classification is complicated but there is a great deal to do without becoming too involved in technical details. Remember, though, children like the sound of words – malachite, quartz, chalcedony and obsidian sound like something from a space fiction story!

People first began to make use of rock when they took shelter in caves and stones were made into edged tools and used for hunting food animals and also as weapons against enemies.

This was in the Stone Age. Humankind has advanced since then and has learned how to use the basic materials found in rocks. These basic materials have remained the same for millions of years.

General notes

1 A rock is a combination of minerals, which are inorganic chemical substances each having definite characteristics.

2 Older children may like to know a little more about rocks generally and can appreciate a broad classification.
a) Igneous rocks – formed when molten rock cools and solidifies (e.g., basalt, granite).
b) Sedimentary rocks – formed when sediment is deposited from water (e.g., limestone, sandstone). This can be shown to them by shaking clay in water and then leaving it to settle.
c) Metamorphic rocks – those changed by heat and pressure (e.g., marble, slate).

3 An ore is a rock or mineral that contains enough of a metal to make it worthwhile extracting for commercial use.

4 Some of the more easily identifiable rocks could be shown to children, named, and their properties discussed.
a) Chalk – sedimentary rock formed in shallow seas from the debris of marine creatures. It is white, evenly grained, soft and crumbly. It contains microscopic fossils. No other rock looks like chalk.
b) Sandstone – sedimentary rock formed from grains of quartz. The grains are visible but bonded together. Its colour varies. It contains fossils and feels rough to the touch. In appearance, it is similar to grit. It is often used in buildings.
c) Granite – igneous rock formed below the earth's surface. It is coarse-grained with visible crystals and is found in many colours (black and white, brown, pink, grey). It is a very hard rock and is used for building.
d) Slate – metamorphic rock formed from volcanic ash under intense pressure. It is smooth, fine grained, and is green, grey, blue or black in colour. Although very hard, it splits easily into thin pieces. No other rock is similar to slate. Its main use is for roofing because it can be split into thin, even slices.

5 Finely broken down rock mixed with organic material forms soil. Topsoil contains rocks and minerals, humus, air, water and living organisms. It may vary in thickness from 2 cm or 3 cm to many centimetres. Below the topsoil are the sub-soil (containing no humus) and the bedrock (see section 16).

Activities and experiments

1 Make a rock and stone collection. It does not matter whether or not specimens are identifiable (though a well illustrated refrence book may help) because children can classify them according to shape, colour, where found, etc.

2 Make specific collections – each one from a limited, but clearly defined area.

3 Look at a collection of named rock specimens. Which names are already familiar to some of the children?

4 Test rocks for hardness by scratching with a nail. (The hardness of minerals is measured on the Moh Scale from 1 to 10. A diamond has a hardness of 10.)

5 Take one type of rock and find out as much about it as possible.

6 Building materials – Look at building materials. How many are made from natural rock, either shaped or left as found? (Cement, concrete, bricks, etc. count as manufactured. Although brick is made from clay, a natural rock, it has been fired, thus altering its composition.) Make a study of walls.

7 History in rocks – The oldest rocks are known to be over 800 million years old, and simple plants and animals first existed about 500 million years ago. Coal seams, formed from plant remains, date from over 300 million years ago, and the first reptiles and mammals appeared about 200 million years ago. Fossils are the remains or prints of plants and animals and are found in rock. Find out about the formation of fossils, and see specimens at local museums. Children may be able to bring some in to school. Make imitation fossils using shells or bones and a mould and cast method.

8 Metals – see section 20.

Useful apparatus

Storage boxes; clay; hammers: protective goggles; sand; cement; modelling clay; plaster of paris; hand lenses; camera; rock collections

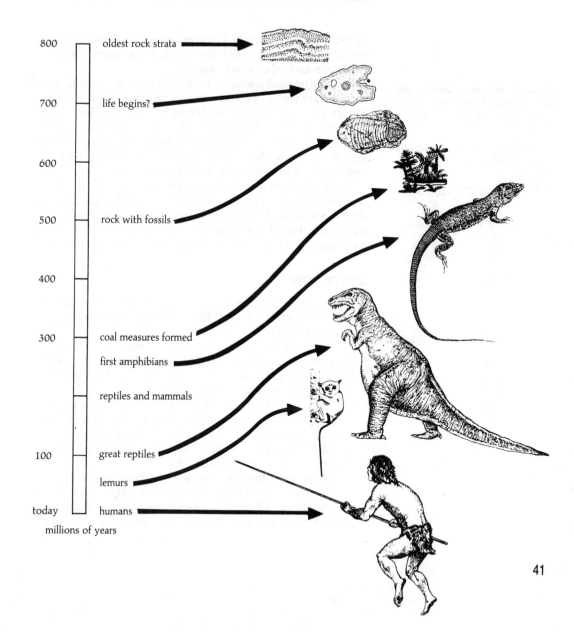

800 oldest rock strata

700 life begins?

600

500 rock with fossils

400

300 coal measures formed

     first amphibians

     reptiles and mammals

100 great reptiles

     lemurs

today humans

millions of years

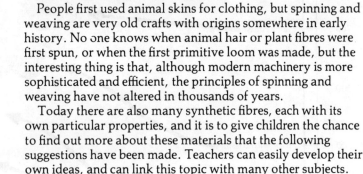

Spinning wool with a hand spindle (a pencil pushed through a potato will make a temporary spindle)

when starting, use wool to make this a piece of knitting loop round wooden weight

Wool, linen, cotton and silk yarns are made of fine natural fibres, twisted together to make yarns. These yarns can be made into knitted or woven fabrics.

People first used animal skins for clothing, but spinning and weaving are very old crafts with origins somewhere in early history. No one knows when animal hair or plant fibres were first spun, or when the first primitive loom was made, but the interesting thing is that, although modern machinery is more sophisticated and efficient, the principles of spinning and weaving have not altered in thousands of years.

Today there are also many synthetic fibres, each with its own particular properties, and it is to give children the chance to find out more about these materials that the following suggestions have been made. Teachers can easily develop their own ideas, and can link this topic with many other subjects.

General notes

1 Fibres are single threads, like a human hair; sheep's wool is best for looking at fibre. The natural fibres come from plant or animal sources:
a) Wool is the most important animal fibre. We usually use the term wool to mean sheep's wool, but other animal fibres can be made into yarns – Angora, cashmere (from a type of goat), camel and alpaca, for example.
b) Cotton and linen are vegetable fibres. Cotton is produced from the seed pod, and each fibre is from 30 to 65 mm long. Linen fibres come from the stem of the flax plant, and each is about 400 to 600 mm long. Linen yarns and fabrics are extremely strong and hardwearing.
c) Other vegetable fibres include jute, hemp and sisal.
d) Silk is an animal fibre. The very fine threads come from the cocoons of silk moths. The history of silk production is a fascinating one, beginning in China about 4600 years ago.

2 It is not easy to identify all the synthetic fibres but these include the polyamides (e.g. nylon), the polyesters (e.g. terylene) and the acrylics (e.g. courtelle and acrilan).

3 The colours of natural fibres are limited, but yarns can be dyed before weaving or printed after being made into fabric.

4 Cloth manufacture –
a) Before making fabric, yarn has to be spun. This was originally done with a spindle, and then later with a spinning wheel. Both have been replaced by complex machinery. To ply the yarn, two or more spun lengths are twisted together.
b) The yarns are woven on some form of loom, and the history of weaving makes an interesting study on its own. To find out more about weaving, look at one of the books suggested in the bibliography.

Activities and experiments

1 Collect as many samples of yarns as possible. Unpick them to see the individual fibres. Identify them, if possible. Test them for strength and elasticity by fixing a length of yarn to a hook, and then putting weights in a bag or net attached at the other end. At what point does the yarn break? (Strength) How much does it stretch? (Elasticity)

2 Fibres twisted together are stronger than fibres on their own. Try twisting fibres of sheep's wool, cotton wool or any other fibre available. Using a simple spindle (see illustration), try spinning some sheep's wool. (Any fleece used by the children should be well washed. To make it easier for them to spin, rub a little cooking oil into it.) To start spinning, loop a piece of knitting wool as shown in the illustration, hold the thread in one hand and twist the spindle with the other; as the fibres

are pulled out, the twist is transferred to them. Try to get someone to demonstrate spinning with a spindle and a spinning wheel.

3 Using any sort of loom, from a board with nails hammered into it to a small table loom, do some simple weaving. Experiment with different yarns in both the warp and weft. Pull fabrics apart to see how they are made. Using large knitting needles and thick wool, knit several rows. This makes a looped fabric. Look how it has been made.

4 Use sheep's wool for experiments with dyeing. Our ancestors used only natural dyes and children can experiment with these. Try boiling the wool with onion skins for an orangey colour, bracken for a yellow-green, elderberries for a pinky-blue. Experiment with other plants. There are many reference books on more complicated dyeing. Historically, wool was the most important fibre in this country.

A plastic seed tray loom. Burn notches at the end with hot wire

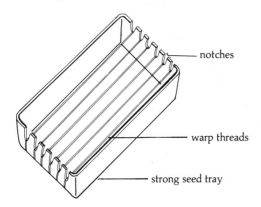

— notches

— warp threads

— strong seed tray

Useful apparatus

Scissors; clamps; net or cloth bags; weights or washers; fleece; spindles (bought or home made); small wooden boxes (for looms; cardboard is not strong enough); pieces of material; large knitting needles; hammer; small nails

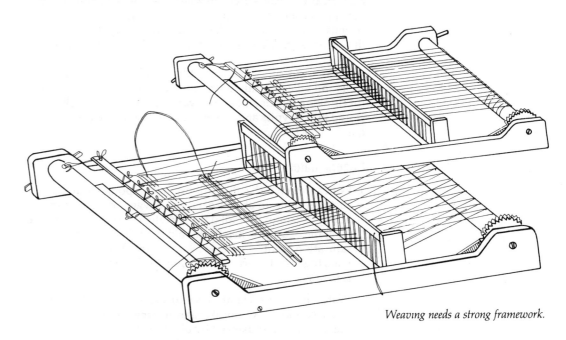

Weaving needs a strong framework.

Water covers about 70 per cent of the earth's surface. Most of it is contained in the oceans and some of it is in a permanently frozen state in the form of glaciers and ice sheets.

Water is essential for all living plants and animals. A reliable water supply was one of the first requisites of settlement. Historically, villages grew up where there was a pond or where the underground supply could be made available using wells or springs. In many parts of the world, this still applies. The drying up of the water supply threatens the lives of people and animals.

In this country, it is still possible to find pumps, troughs, wells and village ponds. Although some spring water is suitable for drinking (and is still used), water for houses is usually stored in reservoirs and is then purified to remove rubbish and harmful bacteria.

General notes

1 Water, which is the most important compound found on earth, is made up of hydrogen and oxygen (H_2O). It can be a liquid, a vapour or a solid (ice). Water constantly evaporates from the oceans. When the humidity of the air reaches saturation point, droplets of water form. These droplets mass together to form clouds, and it is from these clouds that rain falls.

2 Water that falls on land runs into streams (and subsequently into rivers and lakes) or it soaks into the ground, where a great deal of it is taken up by plants.

3 Water dissolves minerals in the rock as it seeps through the ground. Some of these mineral salts (e.g. calcium salts) make it difficult for soap to form a lather; this is termed 'hard' water. Some salts, such as fluorides, are beneficial; fluorides prevent tooth decay.

4 Water normally boils at about 100°C or 212°F. When it boils, it changes into water vapour. It freezes at 0°C and 32°F, and changes into ice. The ice takes up more room than the water from which it has formed. (This is why pipes burst.)

5 Water evaporates all the time, and the rate increases in warm dry conditions. This constant evaporation is responsible for the earth's water cycle (see section 34).

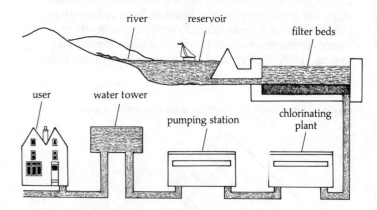

Water's journey from the reservoir to the user

Activities and experiments

1 Uses of water – make a list of all the ways in which water is used in the home, and estimate how much water is used each day.

2 Evaporation – put the same amount of water in several saucers and leave them in different places:
   near an open window in a draught
   outside (if it is not raining)
   in a warm place in the sun or near a radiator
   in a refrigerator
   in a cupboard
   other places suggested by the children

Note how long it takes for the water to evaporate from each saucer.

3 Condensation – look at the condensation formed by steam or by breathing on a cold surface. Investigate conditions needed for condensation.

4 Filtering – water for drinking has to be cleaned and purified (see diagram). Find out how it can be filtered by making a model filter bed.

5 Freezing – put water in various containers, filling to the top, and freeze in a refrigerator. What happens to the water as it freezes? Fill a small, screw-topped plastic bottle. Seal it firmly and freeze it. What happens? (The bottle will either crack or be pushed out at the sides, depending on the strength of the bottle.)

6 Hardness of water – use a bottle that will hold about 500 ml and that has a secure cork or stopper. Mark the bottle about one-third of the way up and fill up to this point with the water to be tested, which must be cold. Add one pinch of soap powder – it must be soap and not detergent – and shake. Does it form a lather that will last for a minute? If so, the water is soft. Go on adding the powder, one pinch at a time, until a lasting lather is formed. Try different types of water (e.g., rain, pond, tap water from different areas, sea water and boiled water) but always use the same amount of cold water. Draw up a chart to show the hardest and the softest waters, and try to answer some questions.

7 Further developments:
   a) Water as a solvent
   b) Distillation
   c) Pollution
   d) Sources of water

Useful apparatus

Plastic bottles; electric kettle; old sheeting; filter paper; paper towels; large flower pots; glass jars and beakers; bricks

Put 1 litre of water in a jar and stick a strip of paper on the outside. Mark the water level each day. Where does the water go?

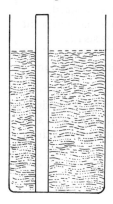

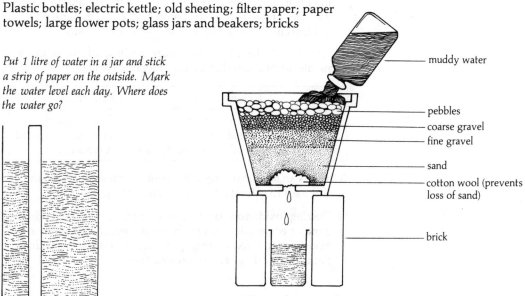

muddy water
pebbles
coarse gravel
fine gravel
sand
cotton wool (prevents loss of sand)
brick

A filter made from a plant pot

It is relatively simple to classify things made of metal, but it is not always easy to identify which metal has been used. Although children like identifying and naming things, it is more important that they become familiar with the general properties of metals first. Then they can find out more about specific metals and how they are used. At this stage, they can also be introduced to the less common metals.

General notes

1 Metals have been known and used for over 5000 years, and those most likely to be known by children are hard, strong, shiny, malleable (can be beaten into sheets), ductile (can be pulled into a wire), and have a high melting point. They will include iron, copper, silver, gold, aluminium and tin. They may also know lead, a dull metal with a low melting point, and mercury, a liquid metal used in thermometers.

2 Some metals are alloys, which are made up of two or more metals, or of a metal and a non-metallic element.

Alloy	Constituents	Properties
Steel	Iron, carbon	Strong, hard
Solder	Lead, tin	Low melting point
Stainless steel	Iron, chromium, nickel	Resists rust

3 Iron is an important metal element. Its ores are abundant and easy to extract. It can be made into steel.

4 Rusting (oxidation) is a feature of iron, and its prevention is a major economic concern. Because oxygen and water are necessary to cause rusting, preventative measures, such as painting or oiling, aim to exclude these.

5 There are many other important metals, including:
Copper – ductile; good conductor of electricity; forms alloys with other metals (bronze with tin; brass with zinc)
Gold – malleable and ductile; easily worked; purity measured in carats (18 carat ring is 18/24 or 75% gold); prized as precious metal
Titanium – extremely strong and light; resists corrosion; increasingly used in aircraft industry

6 Older children may want to know more about the chemistry of metals generally:
a) They are elements or alloys, and most are good conductors of heat and electricity.
b) Most metals occur as ores, and the pure metal has to be extracted from these.
c) Metals have many uses because they are strong, many can be cast, and many have specialized uses. (Tungsten, for example, is used to make electric lamp filaments.)

Using a magnet. This will pick out metals containing iron and steel

Activities and experiments

1 Make a collection of metal objects and try to identify the metal. Find out why this particular metal was used. Why are knives, scissors, needles and many tools made of metal?

2 Make a chart of some of the metals you know, listing their normal uses:

Metal	Uses
Aluminium	Kettles, saucepans, cooking foil
Tin	Coating food containers, alloyed with lead to make solder
Silver	Cutlery, jewellery, also one of the best conductors of electricity

3 Test metals for various qualities:
   a) For hardness. Test by scratching with a sharp nail.
   b) For rusting and oxidation. Wet the metals and leave for two or three weeks. Which metals show signs of oxidation?
   c) For magnetism. Only metals containing iron, nickel or cobalt can be magnetized.
   d) For use in tools. Look at some tools. Find out which metal they are made from, and what job they do.

A thermometer. The metal (mercury) expands in the thermometer

4 Rusting – use nails for this experiment. First find out how long it takes them to rust and then try out ways of preventing rusting, using two or three nails for each test:
   Keep them absolutely dry
   Paint them
   Put them under water
   Cover them with oil
   Wrap them in paper
   Put them in a closed box
   Try out any other suggestions.

5 Show children some mercury. (This must be done by the teacher; the children should not be allowed to touch it.) Show them a large thermometer and explain how it works.

6 Further developments:
   a) Expansion and contraction of metals
   b) The story of the car
   c) Jewellery and metals in art
   d) The Iron and Bronze Ages

Useful apparatus

Files; hammers; nails; oil; grease; needles; scissors; wire; pliers; magnets; thermometers (mercury); samples of metals

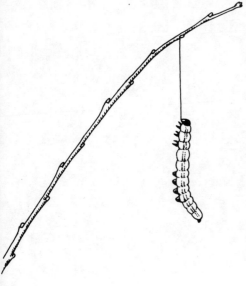

An adhesive is a substance that sticks or adheres to something else. Most children will be inclined to use the words glue or gum though, strictly speaking, glue means an adhesive of animal or vegetable origin, but it hardly matters if children say they glue something together when using a synthetic adhesive. Younger children tend to say they are going to 'stick' something and often assume that any sticky substance can be used for this purpose. This in itself is worth investigating.

The chemistry of adhesives is far too advanced for primary children, but they can learn a lot about simple research by deciding upon ways of testing the usefulness and efficiency of adhesives, and by trying out some old-fashioned recipes. They may even find that some very cheap, easily obtained materials are better for some jobs than bought adhesives.

General notes

1 The cohesion of an adhesive depends largely on the way in which it changes from a liquid or semi-liquid to a solid form. Sometimes adhesives are liquefied by heating, returning to their solid form on cooling. More commonly, an adhesive is dissolved in some sort of solvent. This solvent evaporates into the air, leaving the solid adhesive. Sometimes the solvent is water. Postage stamps have an adhesive that can be softened by wetting the stamp; as the water evaporates, the stamp remains stuck to the envelope.

2 Sometimes two separate liquids are mixed together. These react chemically to form a strong solid.

3 Children will have heard of the 'super' glues. These can be bought quite easily, but should only be used under very strict supervision. Having been told that these adhesives will stick fingers or lips together so that it is impossible to open them, children may be tempted to find out if this is true. It is, so watch carefully against such experiments.

4 There are many uses and types of adhesives. Some are classed as general purpose and some are intended for specific use. There are also adhesive tapes, some used for packaging and some (plasters) for medical use.

Note Some adhesives, notably those containing toluene di-isocyanate (TDI), are associated with glue sniffing. None of these should be used in schools, and no reputable firm should supply these. Do not buy adhesives that do not have their contents clearly marked.

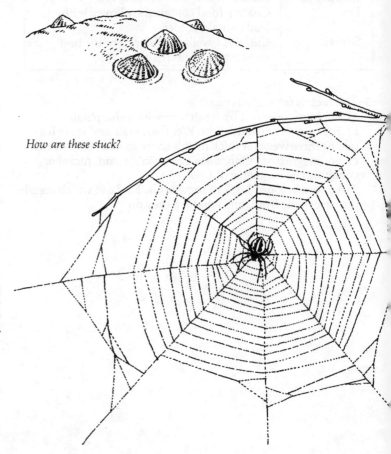

How are these stuck?

Activities and experiments

1 Make as large a collection as possible of adhesives. Read the instructions and note the manufacturer's claims and recommendations. Will each adhesive do what it says provided that the instructions are carried out properly? Is it inflammable? Some claim to stick 'anything to anything'. Do they?

2 Make a chart like the one shown here, and test the adhesives collected.

will it stick?	Glass to glass	Wood to wood	Metal to wood	Paper to wood	Card to glass	Plastic to plastic
Glue A						
Glue B						
Glue C						
Glue D						

3 Test the strength of adhesive hooks of the type used for hanging small kitchen items.

4 Test the strength of different adhesives. In order to compare them, each adhesive must be used on the same type of material and be subjected to the same test. Put weights or washers in a tin and hang it at the bottom of two glued sections (see diagram). At what point do the strips separate? Think of other experiments and use other materials. (Some adhesives are meant for use with certain materials only – rubber, glass, vinyl, etc.)

5 Test wallpaper adhesives.

6 Try substances other than proprietary adhesives and see if they stick. Use treacle, paint, nail varnish, jam, resin, for example.

7 Collect old recipes for home-made glues and test these. Here are some:
a) For flour and water paste, mix a tablespoon of flour with a little water. Add boiling water and stir till it thickens Some people used to use this for wallpaper, but they often added a spoonful of disinfectant. Why?
b) My grandmother replaced a wall tile by painting both the wall and tile with condensed milk, pressing the tile firmly into place, and leaving it untouched for a week
c) This adhesive for mending china was found in an old recipe book. Coat the edges of the broken pieces with egg white and leave to dry. Coat the edges again and stick together. Leave for 48 hours

8 Plants and animals stick to things. Find out how a spider attaches its web, or how a limpet sticks so firmly to rocks. How do plants, such as ivy, stick to walls? The fine filaments of the cocoon of the silk worm are stuck together. Find out more about this.

Useful apparatus

Adhesives of all kinds; wooden lath; small saw; sandpaper; wood drill; string; bean cans; weights; washers or nails; brushes; pieces of leather, glass, plastic, card, fabric, other materials

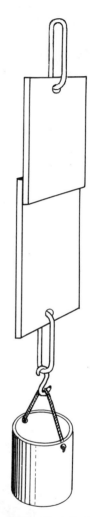

Testing the adhesive power of a glue

Before the invention the wheel, moving large objects such as logs, stones and dead animals must have been extremely arduous with only primitive skids and possibly log rollers.

It is almost impossible for a modern child to imagine life without wheels. They are everywhere: mechanized transport would cease without them and many tools, machines and household items depend on them.

This is a topic for children of all ages and links closely with history, geography and crafts.

General notes

1 The stages at which people began to use the wheel varied from place to place. It is believed that the Sumerians were the first people to use a cart wheel, possibly as early as 4000 years ago. Many pictures on pottery and walls show spoked wheels on chariots from about 3400 years ago. In Britain, the wheel appeared about 2500 years ago, probably brought here by invaders.

2 No one knows just how the wheel was developed, but rollers were almost certainly used first. Since tools were needed to shape the wood into wheels, the invention had to follow knowledge of the use of iron.

3 Other historically useful wheels were the potter's wheel, the waterwheel, the spinning wheel and the windmill. The mechanical clock was first devised in the 13th century and depended on the use of wheels.

4 The wheel improved as passenger transport developed. By the early 17th century, coaches were in regular use and in 1784 light-weight mail coaches were introduced. The bicycle dates from the beginning of the 19th century, and the first were propelled along by pushing on the ground with the feet.

5 The history of the railways is a topic in itself and there are many books on the subject. The same applies to the history of the car, and with this comes the story of the pneumatic tyre. It is fascinating to note that the story goes from ancient times to the present day, and from solid wooden wheels to those capable of carrying Concorde.

Activities and experiments

1 Try using rollers made from pieces of broom handle to move a heavy load – a box of bricks or a wooden box with a child sitting in it.

2 Collect wheeled toys or other examples of things with wheels. Look at the axle at the centre of a wheel. What happens if this is not at the centre?

3 Make models of objects with wheels. Simple carts and trucks and many building toys make this a reasonably simple task. Make a model waterwheel using a cork with pieces of plastic pushed into slots. If a hole has been made through the centre the wheel will turn round a knitting needle as water drips on the blades. Older children can make larger wooden models – barrows, carts, etc.

4 A wheel must grip the ground as it moves round, and this depends on friction between the wheel and the surface. Look at bicycle wheels, car wheels, etc. and find out how well they grip. Why are smooth car tyres dangerous?

5 Make a collection of actual objects, pictures or drawings with specialized wheels. Some of these could be:
Cogs inside a watch or other cogs
Spinning wheel, potter's wheel, tools with wheels
Sewing machine and other machines with wheels
Steering wheel
Furniture castors

6 Work out mathematical problems to do with wheels:
How many times would a bicycle wheel have to go round to get from A to B?
Measure the circumference of a standard car wheel and a mini-wheel. Would the mini-wheel wear out first? How many times must each go round to cover, say, 50 m?
How can a wheel be used to measure the length of the playground? (Use a trundle wheel.)

7 Look at as many wheels as possible so that their importance can be fully appreciated and their use determined: wheelbarrow, bicycle, sewing machine, hand drill, spinning wheel, wheeled toys, others.

8 Further developments:
a) History of the car
b) Story of road travel
c) Making a metal rimmed cart wheel
d) Cog wheels and pulleys

Useful apparatus

Broom handles; saw; strong boxes; building toys; wheeled toys; string; nails; screws; wood; wire; wheels of all sorts

All of these are tools

Children are accustomed to using tools though they may not realize that they are doing so. Almost the first tool that children learn to handle is a spoon, and they quickly learn to use such things as a pencil or a simple digging tool. They push a toy truck round the room on its wheels – these are tools – and see people using hammers, needles, tin openers, scissors, etc. As they develop, they learn to use more and more complex tools and may eventually use the specialized tools of a particular craft or trade.

General notes

1 Tools and machines make work easier. They are used for doing work more efficiently, for moving things with the minimum of effort and for producing the millions of items that are part of everyday living.

2 Basically, tools are specialized for the job they are intended to do. For example:
  a) digging tools – from trowels to road building machinery
  b) cutting tools – knives, axes, scissors, scythes, saws, lawnmowers, metal cutters
  c) drilling tools – hand drills, gimlets, oil drilling equipment
  d) tools for lifting – pulleys, levers, winches, cranes
  e) mixing, crushing and hammering tools – forks, spoons, whisks, electric mixers, concrete mixers, hammers
  f) power tools – those with electric or petrol motors
  g) tools for particular crafts or skills

3 One of the simplest tools is the lever. When we use a spoon handle to work the lid off a tin, we are using a lever. By using a lever, which is pivoted and supported at a point called the fulcrum, less effort is needed.

4 The wheel is an important tool (see section 22), and wheels and levers form the working parts of many machines. Pulleys are wheeled tools used for lifting and hauling.

5 One of the simplest machines is the inclined plane. This is simply a slope for raising loads from one level to another with less effort. A ramp is an inclined plane, and it is obviously far easier to raise, say, a car from one level to another on this than it would be to raise it vertically. It seems likely that stones used for building the pyramids were moved on rollers pushed up earth ramps. A screw is really an inclined plane, but the slope is twisted round the shank of the screw. Run a piece of cotton along the thread from the top to tip and the length of the plane can be seen.

6 Weapons are tools and cannot really be ignored when working with older children. The stress, however, could be on the use of materials – bone, stone, wood, leather, bronze, iron – and could include stone axes, spears, bows and arrows, swords, knives and guns.

Activities and experiments

1 Try to find out all the tools that can be used for:
    carrying
    lifting
    digging, scraping, scooping
    cutting
    boring or grinding
    mixing, blending, stirring
    hammering
    levelling and smoothing
    joining and stitching
    drawing, writing, painting

See or use tools where practical.

2 Look at the tools for particular jobs and, if possible, see them in use or use them. Include such jobs as bricklaying, furniture making, gardening, car maintenance, thatching, knitting, spinning, leather working.

Suitable examples will vary according to the district in which the school is situated.

3 Use toys, such as Meccano, to build cranes and other wheeled items.

4 With a plank of wood at least 1 m long, children can do some work on the use of slopes and ramps. The plank will need raised edges on the long sides. These can be made with strips of thick card glued or tacked to the edge, or wood quadrant can be nailed along the edge. If this is used as a slope (raised on one or two bricks), the children can find out if the incline of the slope makes any difference to the distance travelled by a toy car released at the top of the slope, and can find how much effort is needed to pull the car up the slope. If the slope is put on a table, a string can be attached to the car and run over the end of the slope to hang down. Weights can be tied to the string, so that children can see how many are needed to pull up the car.

5 Friction and movement – see section 25.

6 Children can devise much of their own work on tools and machines, basing it on such things as:
a) The history of tools (and inventing primitive tools such as bone needles)
b) Making a wooden toy (and noting exactly what each tool used does)
c) Making scrap books showing as many tools as they can find.
d) Tools in the home, kitchen, garage, garden, classroom

Useful apparatus

Any tools available; hammers; nails; screwdrivers; screws; wheeled toys; building toys; scissors; glue; sandpaper; tin lids; pieces of wood; inclined plane; oil; marbles; string

Levers make work easier. The bottle and the tin cannot be opened by the fingers alone

There is a great deal of practical work that children can do involving tools, machines and movement. They probably already know something about wheels and simple pulleys, and they will have played with toys that roll and bounce, or are moved by some sort of motor. Without realizing it, they will also have met the effects of friction – when they use the brakes on their bicycles, when a drawer will not pull out easily or when a match is struck on the rough side of a matchbox. Because friction and movement are a feature of everyday life, there are many easily controlled experiments that children can do to find out more about this.

General notes

1 Friction is a force producing resistance when two objects move over or against each other. The rougher the surfaces, the greater the friction. Even apparently smooth surfaces may have some friction because of very small projections inhibiting movement.

2 Friction can cause damage when surfaces rub together. The heat produced can in some circumstances cause serious problems. Some machine tools have to be cooled continuously to prevent the damaging effects of the heat produced by friction.

The hovercraft moves on a cushion of air, minimising the effects of friction

3 Friction can be overcome by using very smooth surfaces, lubricants, wheels, bearings, rollers and air streams (as in the hovercraft). Lubricants separate two surfaces so that projections cannot catch against each other. For example, a stiff hinge moves easily when oiled.

4 Friction can be used to slow down movement and to give grip. Without friction it would be impossible to walk about. Also, it is used in braking and in non-slipping belts on machinery. The tread on tyres provides a grip for the moving vehicle.

5 Friction which prevents movement, such as a handbrake on a parked car, is called static friction. When there is movement with resistance, it is called sliding friction. The force preventing *any* movement of an object, static friction, is greater than the force used for slowing down movement, sliding friction.

Activities and experiments

1 Get children to sandpaper and polish a plank at least
1 m × 20 cm. This can be propped up to make a steep slope.
Bricks are very suitable as props because the angle of the
slope can be easily altered by adding or subtracting bricks.
Slide different objects down the slope and see which go down
easily.

   Having done this, they can undertake more controlled
experiments by using objects of the same size and weight, but
with differing surface finishes. Matchboxes filled with clay or
plasticine can be used to produce uniform blocks, and
different materials (e.g. sandpaper, plastic, rubber, paper,
various fabrics or anything that the children can suggest) can
be stuck on the bottom surfaces. Using the same apparatus,
the children can also find out if weight and size affect the
results.

2 Friction and force – using a smooth, horizontal surface, get
the children to pull a wooden block, with a screw eye for
attachment, across the surface with a strong rubber band.
The stretch of the band will indicate the amount of force
needed to move the block. Different materials can be
attached to the underside to see the effect on the force needed
to move the block. The block must be started in the same
place each time, and the children will need to devise a means
of measuring the amount of stretch. Older children can use a
spring balance.

3 Overcoming friction – the apparatus used in both the
previous experiments can be used to find out if lubricants
will overcome friction. Children can experiment with such
things as butter, water, oil, grease and soap. The friction
boards and other surfaces will need to be cleaned in between
experiments, using a detergent.

4 Friction and heat – children can produce heat through
friction by rubbing their hands together, but they will
probably think that this is simply body heat. A more
convincing action is to rub the bowl of a tablespoon
vigorously on a mat or carpet. The heat produced can be felt
if the spoon is put against the inside of the wrist.

5 Friction is used to slow down movement and to give grip, as
in suitable shoes for running and rubber backed mats to
prevent slipping. Look at floors. Are they safe? Look at
shoes designed for particular use (climbing; football;
ice-skating). Talk about tread and car tyres. How do bicycle
brakes work?

6 Look at friction that is taken for granted without thinking
about it – striking a match; moving heavy furniture; using
scissors (how does oil help if they are stiff?). Test if it is true
that a stiff metal zip fastener can be eased by rubbing it with
pencil lead. Look around for examples of friction.

Useful apparatus

Wooden planks; bricks; boxes; rubber bands; adhesive tape;
sandpaper; rubber and plastic sheeting; wood pieces; saw; oil;
grease; soap

Use the matchboxes to test different surfaces

*Test the use of oil or grease for reducing friction (grease the
bottom of the brick). How many weights are needed to move
it – before and after greasing?*

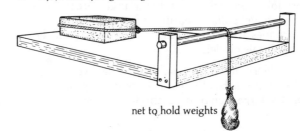

net to hold weights

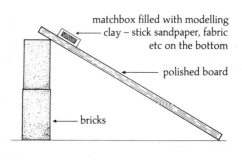

matchbox filled with modelling
clay – stick sandpaper, fabric
etc on the bottom

polished board

bricks

55

From the moment infants begin to place one brick on top of another, they are involved with structure. When the whole thing topples over because the bricks have not been aligned, they are learning something about the construction of buildings and bridges.

As children get older, they will see all around them examples of girders, frames, arches, towers and walls. They will see different types of bridges, scaffolding and cranes. There are structures built by people everywhere. All of these have had to be made out of suitable materials and in such a way that they are appropriate for their particular use.

General notes

1 When any material is compressed or pulled by equally opposing forces, it is under stress. This causes materials to bend or, if too strong, to break. Tubing will stand greater stress than flat strips, so a bicycle frame is made of metal tubing.

2 The change of shape of a material caused by stress is called strain. When structures are being designed, the effects of all the forces they will be subjected to have to be allowed for and the materials used have to be strong enough to withstand them. The strain caused by two equal forces pushing together is compression, while that caused by forces pulling apart is tension.

3 Many structures such as bridges and cranes have the framework joined in such a way that triangles are formed. Rectangular shapes collapse easily under stress, but triangular shapes are much stronger. This can be seen very easily using simple models.

4 Arches help distribute the load so that it is carried by the sides of the supports, but there is a tendency to push outwards. On large arch bridges, this is overcome by

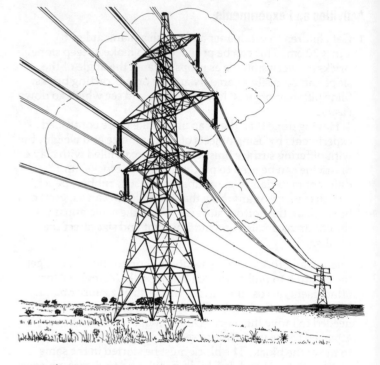

building abutments at either end; these need to be large and heavy enough to counteract the outward thrust.

5 Bridges are specialized structures – see section 26.

6 Buildings and other structures make use of many different materials. Again, this could form the basis of a group or class project. Examples of different types of materials include:

a) Natural stone – either as it is found or shaped in some way. This includes slate, once an important roofing material but less used these days.

b) Bricks – manufactured stones, cuboid in shape but of many different types
c) Concrete and mortar
d) Metal – steel girders and frameworks, reinforced concrete, window frames
e) Wood
f) Other materials – plastics, glass, plaster, cement, putty, paint

Activities and experiments

1 All sorts of structures can be made with drinking straws joined by soft wire. If the children want to make larger structures, they can use tubes made out of sheets of newspaper. (If six or more pages are rolled up tightly and then rolled in a further sheet that has been pasted all over, the result, when dry, will be a firm tube of paper.) Can the children make a structure that will test the strength of such tubes? Using newspaper tubes, is it possible to make a structure that will support a child?

2 Using wooden, metal or plastic strips, join four pieces to form a rectangle. This can be pushed out of shape quite easily, but if another piece is added so that it forms a diagonal and makes two triangles, the shape remains rigid. This is a very simple model. More complicated ones can be made and the children will devise these for themselves if given the materials.

3 If three bamboo poles are joined at the top so that a tripod is produced, the children will find that it collapses if they lean on it. But if they make a triangular base, with a leg attached to each angle, the structure is then extremely rigid and will withstand a lot of pressure.

4 Test the breaking stress of various materials using strips, rods and tubes of wood, plastic, metal, card. Resting the ends on two chairs or on bricks, hang a small plastic bucket in the middle and put weights in it. Are strips or rods stronger? Is a tube stronger than a solid bar? Test various tubes. Test the vertical strength of tubes by standing them on end and putting weights on top. Is it possible to make tubes that will support a person? Try this by making tubes from pieces of card, all the same size, stuck with adhesive tape. Stand these up and put a piece of wood on top. Find out how many are needed to support one person's weight.

5 Several experiments can be carried out to compare the properties of different materials.
a) Find out the difference between cement, concrete and mortar.
b) The children can test different mixes of concrete, which is made up of sand, cement and gravel. This can be done by casting small beams in a mould and testing them in the same way as they tested tubes. Concrete for beams is normally one part cement, two parts sand and four parts gravel mixed with enough water to make a stiff consistency.

6 Further developments:
a) Waterproofing of buildings
b) Building tools
c) Interesting structures (domes, drilling rigs, steeples, cranes, etc.)

Useful apparatus

Housebricks; wooden bricks; wood; card; string; construction toys; modelling clay; straws; wire; newspapers; glue; toy cars; weights; small boxes; drawing pins; paper fasteners; clamps

A piece of card (about 20 cm × 9 cm) can be folded in different ways to show that strength also depends on shape (girders etc)

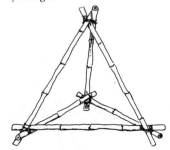

Build rigid structures – making use of triangles

57

The very first bridge was probably a tree trunk that had fallen accidentally over a stream. From this it was only a short step to the deliberate dragging of logs or stones to make the crossing of small waterways quicker, safer and easier.

From these very humble beginnings stem all the bridges that can be seen today. Some of these are very simple, and some are magnificent feats of engineering skill, but there is a fascination about bridges that children usually respond to. Bridges can be looked at, not only as structures, but also as part of the environment.

General notes

1 Bridges are of four main types:
  a) Beam bridge – in its simplest form, this is a plank laid across a stream, supported only at each end. A long, flat bridge has a tendency to bend in the middle and, if the stress is too great, the bridge could break. To overcome this, beam bridges are often built with several supports, reducing the length of any section. One example is the Britannia Bridge over the Menai Straits in North Wales.
  b) Arch bridge – in its modern concrete form, this is seen over many motorways. A famous arch bridge is the Sydney Harbour Bridge in Australia.
  c) Cantilever bridge – this is made of two beams, each supported at one end. The Forth Railway Bridge in Scotland is an example of a large cantilever bridge.

d) Suspension bridge – this consists basically of a track supported by cables slung between the two ends. Very primitive suspension bridges made of rope have been used for hundreds of years, but a modern bridge has steel cables slung between towers. They are stronger than they look, although there can be considerable movement. The Clifton Suspension Bridge, Bristol, will move as much as 30 cm up and down in a high wind.

There are many bridges that are variations of the main types. There is quite a lot of work possible in looking at bridges or pictures of them, and trying to decide what type of bridge each one is. It is interesting that Tower Bridge, London has cantilevered arms which can move up and down.

2 Some of the work on bridges could include their history and a look at famous bridges of the world.

3 Depending on the age of the children involved, they could look at the forces within the structures. (A force is anything that can act on a stationary body and make it move, so forces must act in opposition to each other to keep a body in one place. All forces are pushes, pulls or twists, and one force must be balanced by another.

Different types of bridges

stepping stones

clapper bridge

packhorse bridge

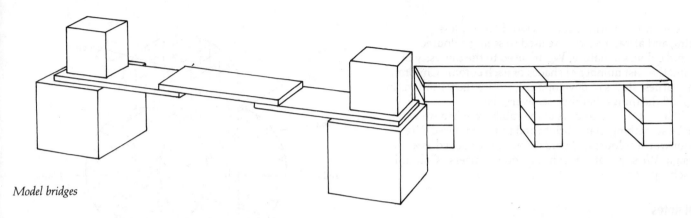

Model bridges

Activities and experiments

1 Make a survey of all the bridges in the neighbourhood. Classify them according to:
a) Type
b) The materials from which they are built
c) Use
d) Age and history, if available

2 Make model bridges. These should be strong enough to hold toy cars.
a) A simple beam bridge can be made by using house bricks for end supports and a strip of wood or card for the roadway. This is adequate for a short span. A longer one will need either more pillar supports or angled supports from the sides, making triangles.
b) Make a simple arch bridge (see the diagram).
It is not easy to make an arch with a keystone but is worth trying. The building blocks can be made from modelling clay or cut from polystyrene block.
c) A simple cantilever bridge can be made by holding down the two ends with weights (see the diagram). In constructing a real bridge, parts are built out from each shore first. A long bridge, such as the Forth rail bridge, requires building land masses like islands because the two shores are too far apart for one span.
d) Children can devise ways of constructing a model suspension bridge remembering that the roadway is suspended from cables attached at each end.
e) Make other models based on bridges seen or known by the children. They are probably familiar with Tower Bridge which is a bascule type. How about the swing bridge, pontoon bridge, toll bridge?

3 Make a study of rail bridges, motorway bridges or river bridges.

Useful apparatus

House bricks; wooden bricks; thick card; wooden strip; glue; string; wire; match boxes; polystyrene block; modelling clay; plastic and metal meccano

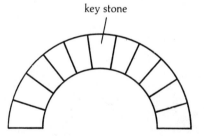

key stone

Pattern for making an arch bridge

Without colour the world around us would be far less interesting and attractive. We are used to seeing coloured objects and colours in nature. We are used to the diversity of colour and the vast number of shades of each colour. Children, from the earliest stages of development, notice the variations in colour of all the things that they see every day.

We talk about 'all the colours of the rainbow' when we want to describe something that is bright and multi-coloured. We talk about warm colours and cold colours. We use red as a danger sign. We say that someone has 'green fingers'. Colour is very much a part of life.

General notes

1 A beam of light – white light – appears to be colourless, but it can be broken down into a sequence of colours called the spectrum. In 1666 Sir Isaac Newton showed that, if a beam of light is passed through a glass prism, it splits into seven colours – red, orange, yellow, green, blue, indigo and violet. White light is, then, a mixture of colours.

2 The colours in a rainbow are the same as in the spectrum. Rainbows occur when the sun shines after rain showers because the raindrops suspended in the atmosphere act as prisms.

3 Primary colours are those which cannot be made by mixing other colours. The primary colours of light (seen, for example, in theatre lighting) are green, blue and red. White is a combination of all three. The primary colours of paint are yellow, red and blue. These three together form black.

4 Animal camouflage depends on colour. The stripes of the tiger blend with the light and shadows of the jungle, and the spotted upper-surface of the plaice makes it almost invisible

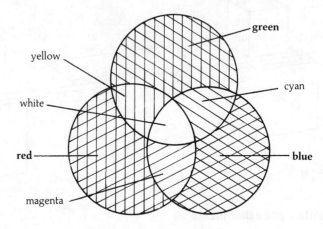

The primary colours of light are red, green and blue.

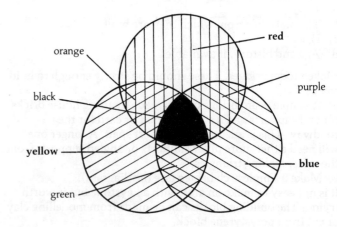

The primary colours of paint are yellow, red and blue

on the sandy seabed. Some animals change colour so that they blend into their surroundings. Sometimes this change is fairly rapid (the octopus and the chameleon) and sometimes it is seasonal (the browny-red stoat which changes to white in winter in northern countries). The frog's skin will vary from green to brown, according to its habitat.

5 Among mammals only the primates (humans, apes and monkeys) can appreciate colour. Butterflies are probably able to distinguish colours, but different species react to different ones. Bees are sensitive to certain colours, though apparently blind to red. Some people are colour blind. Their eyes are not sensitive to one or more of the primary colours. The commonest form of colour blindness is the inability to distinguish red and green.

Activities and experiments

1 Start by simply looking at colours. Collect objects of one colour and note all the possible shades. Choose, say, green and make a shades chart by mixing green paint with black and/or white paint. Do this fairly systematically by adding one drop at a time to the green.

2 Look at light passing through a prism. If a glass prism is not available, let sunlight pass through a jar of water standing on white paper. This works better with a single ray of light (see the diagram).

3 Try mixing colour using spinners made from a circle of card on a stick or pencil. Colour the circle in segments of red and blue, and see what happens when it is spun. Try this with other colours.

4 Mix colours with paints to find out what various combinations make. For example:
   Red and blue make?
   Blue and green make?
   Red and green make?
   Yellow and red make?

5 Find the answers to various problems:
   Which colours used for decorating a room are warm colours? Which are cold?
   Devise a test to find out which coloured flowers insects like best
   Using paints, how would you make beige, purple, navy blue, or pink?
   After green, what is the commonest natural colour?

6 Further developments :
   a) Animals and colour
   b) Colour blindness
   c) Camouflage
   d) Colour changes (in autumn, fruit ripening, dyeing, fading)
   e) Visibility and colour (safety clothing; notices; traffic lights)

Useful apparatus

Paints; crayons; coloured acetate sheet; paint brushes; dyes; prisms; card; transparent materials; coloured wools; torch; bun tins (for paint blending); paint sample cards (from the decorators); glass jar

A jar prism

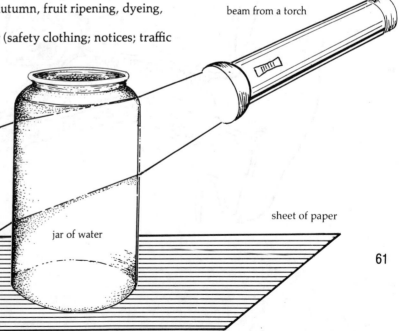

beam from a torch

sheet of paper

jar of water

rainbow colours

We are surrounded by sounds from the moment we are born, and it is only the profoundly deaf that fail to react in some way. Being aware of sound doesn't necessarily mean that we are listening. We are so used to the constant output from radio, television and traffic, for example, that we are often unaware of what is actually going on. There can be so much noise in a busy street that the individual sounds are virtually obliterated. In an active classroom, children often have to be taught to listen.

They need to be made aware of the wide variation of sounds, and to realize that these can be pleasant or unpleasant, relaxing or disturbing. It is only by listening that children will find the sounds that please them.

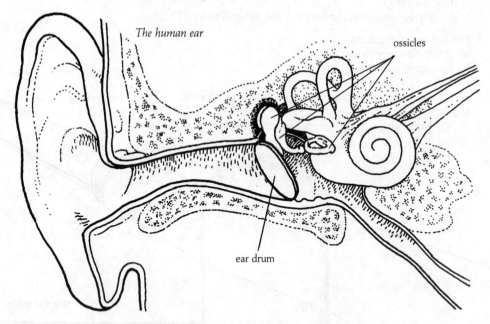

The human ear

ossicles

ear drum

General notes

1 Sound is produced by vibrations that cause waves to spread outwards from the source of the sound. Sound must have a medium through which to travel and this medium can be air, liquid or a solid. It cannot travel through a vacuum.

2 Sound travels in air at a speed of approximately 1120 feet per second.

3 The more vibrations a second, the higher will be the note produced; fewer vibrations give lower notes. This is called the pitch of a note. Loudness depends on the intensity of the sound, and differs from pitch. A note can be loud and high pitched, loud and low pitched, etc.

4 If a sound bounces back, it is called an echo. Sound bounces off hard surfaces (rock and walls) better than it does off soft surfaces (curtains and carpets). This has to be taken into consideration in concert halls and recording studios.

5 Regular vibrations produce musical notes and pleasant sounds and irregular vibrations produce noise. Noise is measured in decibels. The noise of two people talking quietly is about 20 decibels. A noise of 120 decibels is so loud that it can cause actual physical pain.

6 Sound is heard through the ears. The normal ear is extremely sensitive and can pick up very soft sounds. Animals may have ears even if they are not external. The ear openings of birds lie under the feathers behind the eyes. The frog has exposed eardrums at the side of the head. A fish has nerve cells running along each side, which are sensitive to vibrations, although they cannot hear in the way that birds and mammals can.

Activities and experiments

1 Some of the basic work on sound can include:
   Listening to the sounds all around and identifying these
   Listening to a prepared tape of sounds
   Collecting sound words – these may be onomatopoeic or descriptive
   Making sounds using the body only – clapping, scratching, whistling

2 Find out if sound can travel through wood, water, brick or the ground. Get the children to suggest ways of doing this. Here are some examples:
   a) Putting an ear against the wall and asking someone to tap on the other side
   b) 'Listening' to a watch through a long piece of dowel
   c) Ringing a bell inside a tank of water

3 Make a string and food tin telephone (see diagram). Why does this work?

4 A stethoscope can be made with two plastic funnels and a length of plastic tubing. The heartbeat can be heard if one end is put against a child's chest, and another child listens through the second funnel.

5 Devise experiments to find out how far sound travels. (An alarm clock with a loud tick is useful for these experiments.)

6 Investigate the source of sound. Can children accurately locate where a sound is coming from? Test this using a bell or other instrument. One child is blindfolded, and has to say where another child, who is ringing the bell, is standing.

7 Make simple musical instruments, such as shakers made from two yoghurt pots taped together with rice inside; beer can drums; milk bottle xylophone.

8 Find out more about ears. Animal ears come in many shapes and sizes. Are there any reasons for this? Let the children look at their own ears. Find out more about the structure of ears, and discuss the importance of being able to hear. Talk, too, about deafness and the use of deaf aids to help with hearing.

Useful apparatus

Plastic funnels; plastic tubing; rubber bands; dried peas; rice; alarm clock; dowel; toys that make sounds; empty tins (remove both ends without leaving sharp edges); yoghurt containers; string; tape recorder; spoons; real musical instruments

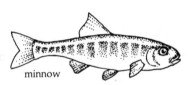

minnow

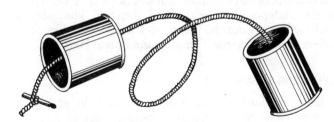

mouse

toad

robin

Ears and hearing. The mouse's ears are obvious, but can the others hear?

A string telephone made from two tins (with the tops taken off so that there are no sharp edges), long piece of string (10–15m) and two matchsticks. Make a small hole in the bottom of each tin.

63

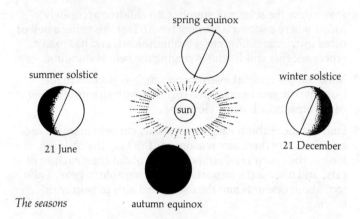

The seasons

Children gradually become aware of units of time because of the regular events that take place. They get up in the morning and go to bed at night; at midday they have their dinner; once a week they go to grandma's to tea. Passage of time is measured by the sequence of happenings within a given period – get up, have breakfast, go to school, have milk, etc.

At a fairly early age they notice that watches and clocks are used by people to 'tell the time'. They accept these conventional timers as a part of everyday life, but it is possible for them to use other timing devices to indicate the interim between two events.

General notes

1 Early peoples must have judged time from the recurrence of night and day and the changing seasons. Perhaps they also noticed that the moon changed shape regularly, and that the sun appeared to move across the sky. Also, the ebb and flow of the tide occurred regularly and rhythmically.

2 The length of a day (24 hours) is the time taken for the earth to rotate on its own axis. A month approximates to the time taken for the moon to move around the earth – this is about 29½ days. A year is the time taken by the earth to travel round the sun, and this takes 365 days, 5 hours, 48 minutes, 46 seconds. This is obviously an inconvenient length of time, so a year is considered to be 365 days long and an extra day is added every four years to account for the odd hours.

3 Clocks are very old. The ancient Egyptians used shadow and candle clocks, and the earliest known sundial was probably made over 3000 years ago. Water clocks (clepsydra), which do not have to rely on the sun, are as old as shadow clocks. Sand and candle clocks were used to indicate definite passages of time, such as the interval between different offices in monasteries. It is not known who made the first mechanical clocks, but they all contain three main parts:

Driving mechanism – a falling weight, a spring, a motor, etc.
Regulating mechanism – a pendulum or balance spring
Escapement – a device linking the driving and regulating mechanisms, and governing the speed of rotation of the hands of the clock

The first clocks had no hands, but struck the hours and the quarters; later one hand was added, then two. The history of clocks will introduce children to such names as Galileo, Robert Hooke, Thomas Tompion and Robert Harrison.

Activities and experiments

1 Collect time words such as second, minute, hour, spring, summer, week, month, century, yesterday, tomorrow, decade, era, night, day, a.m., p.m.

2 Discuss, and find, biological clocks:
   Opening and shutting of flowers (e.g. daisy)
   Bird roosting and migration
   Nocturnal animals, waking at dusk
   Seasonal changes in plants and animals

3 Making timers:
   a) Sand timer – use dry salt instead of sand. Fill a dry washing-up liquid bottle with salt, and invert over a narrow glass jar. Graduate the jar and use as an arbitrary timer.
   b) Water timer – make a small hole in a plastic bottle so that water drips out. Either graduate the bottle or the jar into which it drips.
   c) Candle clock – see diagram.
   d) Shadow clock – only useful on sunny days! The simplest is a length of dowel held upright in a pot filled with sand or stones (see the diagram). The position of the shadow can be chalked on the ground every hour. Look, too, at a real sundial and see if the children can decide why this has limited use.

Discuss how this sundial could be used to tell the time. Why would it be useless at night?

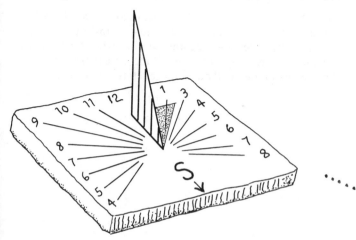

4 Use a stop clock to do some accurate timing: how far does a snail move in one minute? What is your pulse beat per minute? (Push a drawing pin into a drinking straw so that the straw is horizontal. If the head of the drawing pin is placed over the wrist pulse, the movements of the straw can be counted.)

5 Problem solving – these can vary according to the age of the children: How many bricks can you put in the box while the sand timer runs through? If there were no clocks, how would you know when to go to bed? Every day the tide goes in and out. Are there other things that happen every day?

6 Pendulums can be made with weights hung on string. If the length of the string is altered, it can be seen that the pendulum will swing at a different rate – the shorter the string the greater number of times the pendulum will swing in a minute. One swing is counted when the pendulum swings forward and back to the start. If a washing-up liquid bottle is cleaned and thoroughly dried, it can be filled with salt and suspended upside down. As it swings the salt will trace out patterns onto a sheet of black paper underneath.

Measuring time

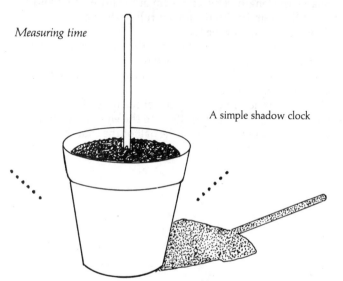

A simple shadow clock

Useful apparatus

Plastic bottles particularly washing-up liquid bottles; jars; candles; thread; drawing pins; dowel; flower pots; card; corks; nails; string; table salt; sand; old clocks and watches; seconds timer.

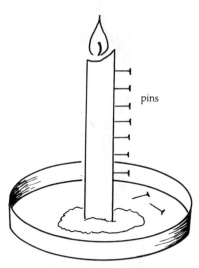

pins

A candle clock – fix to tin lid with modelling clay

65

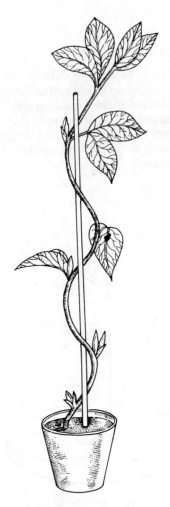

The clockwise spiral of the runner bean

Most children are introduced to various measurements based on the body at some time and know how to measure a yard from the fingers of an outstretched arm to the tip of the nose. They may even know that Goliath, whose height according to the bible was six cubits and a span, must have been a giant (about 3 m tall).

Mathematically and historically, these are interesting facts, but there are many other aspects of mathematics and biology that will interest children and will be worth investigating. They will not only learn more about living organisms, but they will also have to cope with some quite difficult calculations and mathematical concepts. This work can be adapted to almost any age and ability, and many of the problems can be made sufficiently difficult to stretch even the brightest child.

General notes

1 Historically, length was measured using various parts of the adult body. Children will realize very quickly how unsatisfactory such measurements must have been. Examples include:

  Span – the length between the tip of the little finger and the tip of the thumb with the fingers fully extended
  Foot – the length of the foot
  Yard – distance between the tip of the nose and the fingers with the arm stretched out sideways
  Fathom – length from finger tip to finger tip with the arms stretched out sideways
  Hand – distance across the palm at the base of the fingers
  Cubit – distance from the elbow to the end of the fingers
  Inch – possibly the width of the ball of the thumb

2 Animals move in different ways and at different speeds. Facts about animal speeds can be looked up. (A cheetah can move at almost 113 kph.) Children can measure the speed of snails, woodlice and earwigs.

3 Spirals can be found in both plants and animals. For example, in shells, the horns of some animals, climbing plants (stems and tendrils), the arrangement of leaves on stems, and fir cones.

4 The hexagonal cells of a honeycomb fit together – that is, they tesselate. By building triangular, square and hexagonal containers – each with the same height and perimeter – it can be shown that the hexagonal box will hold the most honey.

5 Animals and many plant forms are symmetrical. The importance of symmetry in animal bodies can be seen when looking at movement, flight, etc.

Activities and experiments

1 Children can look at the use of the body as a basis for units of measurement and can decide how accurate these measurements are likely to be. They can talk about the importance of standard measures.

2 The rates at which animals travel can be compared, and children can make a chart of records – the fastest moving animal, the slowest moving animal, the fastest bird in flight, the fastest racehorse. They cannot measure these for themselves so they will have to use reference books.

3 The speeds of small animals (ants, earwigs, woodlice, centipedes, snails, caterpillars, beetles) can be measured by timing how long it takes the animal to move a set distance (say 25 cm). The trouble is that it is hard to get an animal to move in a straight line!

4 The rate of growth can be looked at. Pea or bean plants grown in pots can be measured weekly; plants grown in different conditions can be compared. Do pea plants grow more in hot or cold conditions, in sun or shade, in dry or wet conditions?

5 Collect samples of clockwise and anti-clockwise spirals. Examples: water and land snail shells; animal horns (pictures); climbing plants (stems and tendrils). In which direction do the stems usually spiral? Can they be made to change direction?

6 Look for symmetry; find the lines of symmetry. Discuss why it is necessary for an animal body to be symmetrical.

7 Problem solving involving both mathematics and biology
a) A mouse can eat its own weight in food every day. Do you, or could you, do this? If a mouse is weighed, a packet of food of the same weight can be shown. A child can also be weighed and food equal to his or her weight can be collected. (The smallest child in the class should be chosen for this.)
b) How much water does a plant absorb in one day?
c) How strong is a limpet shell?
d) Are leaves all arranged on stems in the same way? Look at the ways in which they spiral round the stem. Make a model to show this and find out the pattern of the arrangement.
e) Do shape and size affect the way an animal moves, and the speed at which it moves?

Useful apparatus

Seconds timer; mirrors; corks; dowel; seed trays; plant pots; pea and bean seeds; hand lenses; card; glue; shells; tape measures

Lines of symmetry through a leaf, an insect and a mouse

Leaf arrangement on a stem — a model made with paper leaves, dowel and a cork

fur and wool

feathers

hibernation

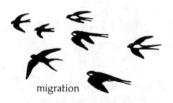

migration

Keeping warm in winter

It is quite obvious that temperature changes according to the season, and that it is colder in winter than it is in summer. Children readily appreciate that they need warmer clothes when playing in the snow, and that it can sometimes be difficult to keep cool on a hot sunny day.

They can look at the ways in which we, and other animals, cope with the variation of temperature.

General notes

1 Dark dull surfaces are good absorbers of heat, but light shiny surfaces absorb very little. Black polythene sheeting, used by gardeners to cover such things as strawberry beds, absorbs available heat and warms the soil underneath.

2 Bright shiny surfaces reflect heat. Electric fires often have bright metal surfaces behind the source of heat so that the heat is reflected into the room. In hot countries, houses painted white keep cooler because heat is reflected and not absorbed. Similarly, light clothes tend to be cooler than dark ones.

3 Heat is passed through matter by conduction. If we want to prevent heat loss we need to use bad conductors (or insulators). Metals are very good conductors of heat, so a saucepan with a solid metal handle will get too hot to pick up. If it has a wooden or plastic handle (poor heat conductors) it can be used safely.

4 Air is a very poor conductor of heat, so materials which trap air will keep heat in. Examples are:
    Birds' feathers and woollen clothes (air is trapped between the fibres)
    Expanded polystyrene and fibreglass used for house insulation
    Double glazed windows (air is trapped between panes)

5 Cool clothes are thin to reduce the amount of air trapped between the fibres, light-coloured to reflect heat and not absorb it, and will leave areas of skin exposed so that sweat evaporates quickly. (Evaporation helps cool the skin.) In very sunny conditions, however, the skin has to be covered to prevent burning.

6 Mammals and birds are warm-blooded and maintain a constant body temperature, so they need to be able to retain heat in cold conditions and to lose heat in hot conditions. Several examples of adaptations exist:
a) Animals living in a very cold climates are usually large with a proportionately small surface area in relation to their body weight (e.g. polar bears and reindeer).
b) An elephant is a very large animal living in a hot climate. To give a greater surface area for heat loss, its skin hangs in folds and it has large floppy ears.
c) Very small animals with a large surface area in proportion to the body weight usually live in warm climates or hibernate in winter (e.g. harvest mice).
d) Animals such as dogs lose excess heat from their tongues when panting and also from the bottom of their feet. It is interesting to note that polar bears have a layer of hair on their feet which helps them to retain heat as well as to move over frozen surfaces.

Activities and experiments

1 Look at coverings. Make a study of animal coverings (perhaps after a zoo visit) and look at clothing suitable for different conditions.

2 Absorbers of heat – two food tins can be used for this study. Paint one with a dull black paint and leave the other shiny. Inside each tin stick a twopence coin with a blob of candle wax. If both tins are stood at an equal distance from a source

of heat, with the twopences towards the heat, it can be seen that the coin in the black tin falls first. A radiator or hot water pipe will provide sufficient heat if the tins are placed about 10 cm away. Having tried this, the children can experiment with different surfaces – painted white, covered tightly with different coloured papers.

3 Older children can be taught to use thermometers so that more accurate measurements can be made. Find out how well different materials will keep in heat by filling a tin with hot water and taking the temperature. Completely cover the tin with the material to be tested and leave for an hour. Take the temperature again. Compare the insulating properties of different materials.

4 Younger children can do a similar experiment using a hot-water bottle filled with hot water. Cover this with the material to be tested and put an ice cube on top. How quickly does it melt?

    Note   All tests must be done at the same room temperature, so it is better to test three or four examples at the same time, subjecting them to the same conditions.

5 Give the children problems to solve so that they can devise their own experiments. Examples are:

a) If you place your hand flat against a metal surface, why does it feel colder than when you put your hand on a polystyrene tile or a piece of wood?

b) Newspaper can be wrapped around things to keep them cold (such as a block of ice cream), but will it also help to keep things hot?

c) Why does a thick, hairy woollen coat keep you warmer than a thin smooth one?

d) Find out about 'survival bags'. Climbers and walkers carry these. Why?

e) Why can a polar bear survive arctic conditions and not a rabbit?

f) How do animals living in very hot climates keep cool?

g) How can you keep cool on a very hot day?

h) How does hibernation help some animals to live through the winter?

6 Think up some experiments to test the suitability of cool or hot weather clothing. Here are two examples:

    Wear two different types of gloves or socks and see which is the warmest or coolest?

    Find which colours absorb the most heat by wrapping tins of cold water in, say, coloured jumpers and placing these about 10 cm from a radiator.

7 Why do you feel hot in an overheated room? Find out about suitable temperatures for working in.

Useful apparatus

Thermometers; empty tins; hot water bottles; samples of different fabrics; examples of clothing; polystyrene tiles; matt black paint; coins; old mail order catalogues (for pictures of clothing); ice; electric kettle (for teacher's use)

Warm-blooded animals

Cold-blooded animals

Testing the insulating powers of materials. The syrup tin is filled with hot water and covered with the material to be tested

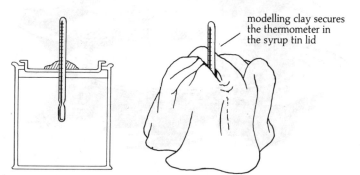

modelling clay secures the thermometer in the syrup tin lid

Most of the things that children find out about the world around them are the result of actual experience and, in the present day, they are surrounded by scientific discoveries. Television, radio, aeroplanes, space travel and the exploration of oceans are all taken for granted. Experimenting with mirrors may therefore seem a long way from atomic submarines, but learning about reflection is important and provides the foundations for later work.

Very young children are not going to be able to understand the science of light, but they can find out about reflective surfaces, and the older children can look further into the use and science of mirrors.

General notes

1 Reflections can be seen wherever there is a smooth, shiny surface, such as glass and steel mirrors, tin cans, shiny spoons and knives, polished copper and brass, highly polished furniture, puddles and pools.

Reflection in water

this is mirror writing

Mirror writing

2 A flat mirror is called a plane mirror. The image seen in it is laterally inverted, that is, changed from side to side. If you raise your right hand, the image in the mirror appears to raise its left hand. It is also the same size as the object that is being reflected, and looks as if it is as far behind the mirror as the object is in front of it.

3 Shiny curved surfaces distort the image. In a convex mirror, such as the back of a spoon, the image is small, clear and the right way up. This makes it useful as a car mirror and a dentist's mirror. A concave mirror is one that is hollowed like the bowl of a spoon. When close to a concave mirror, the image is large and the right way up. Shaving and make-up mirrors are usually concave.

4 Mirrors have many uses apart from the obvious one of reflecting our images: for example, on a microscope, as a light reflector; used decoratively to give an impression of space; distorting mirrors at fun fairs; simple periscopes; placed to show the back of an exhibit in a museum.

5 If two mirrors are placed at an angle with an object between them, the number of images seen depends on the angle of the mirrors. If the mirrors are placed parallel to each other, then any object placed between them is reflected a great number of times.

Activities and experiments

1 Investigate reflective surfaces such as shiny tins, spoons, knives, metal foil, shiny tiles, pool of water, dark glass bottle, glass and metal mirrors.

2 Look at the reflection in a mirror. Is it an exact reflection of, say, a child's face? With older children, find out about lateral inversion. Look at writing in the mirror. What happens? Is it possible to make the reflected writing readable?

3 Find out other ways in which mirrors are used: for example, by dentists; on cars; on dangerous bends in the road; in toys such as kaleidoscopes.

4 Experiment using two or more mirrors. What happens to reflections of an image when two mirrors are placed at an angle? Find out how two mirrors can be used to see the back of the head. Place mirrors so that you can see round corners. Find out what a periscope is. Make a model periscope (see diagram). Find out what a camera obscura is. (There is a very fine one in Edinburgh.)

5 Place a plane mirror in a stand. Shine a narrow beam of light into it. (Use a torch, covering the front with a piece of black paper with a slit cut in it.) What happens?

6 Look at reflections in curved surfaces. If real mirrors are not available, polish metal spoons and use both sides of these. Find out about these reflections.

7 It is not easy to make a mirror. A real mirror is made with silvered glass backed with dark varnish or paint. Children can try to make mirrors with metal foil or polished cans.

8 Investigate 'mirror' symmetry.

Useful apparatus

Mirrors of all sorts (stick masking tape over the backs so that all the pieces will hold together if they are broken); stands for mirrors (modelling clay; corks with slits cut in them) metal spoons; tins; metal polish; metal foil; any shiny surfaced objects; torches (It is possible to buy plastic mirror material, which can be cut with scissors, from school suppliers. This is useful for making curved mirrors.)

Look in one mirror and you will see one reflection: if you put a pencil in front of a mirror, you will see one pencil in the mirror. If you look in two mirrors, you will see a number of reflections

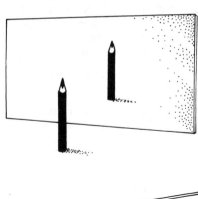

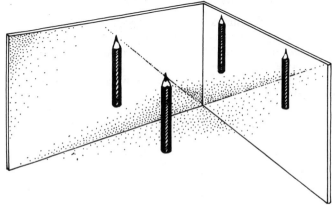

71

Air is all around us, and children are well aware of this. They will glibly tell you that you have got to breathe air or you would die, but they seem to be unsure as to whether air is really 'something'. Older children will understand that an empty bottle is not actually empty, but contains air, although they cannot see it and they do not know how they can demonstrate that it is there. Once children realize that air exists and occupies space, they will find it much easier to appreciate the properties of air and the uses to which it can be put.

General notes

1 Air has definite properties. It is a gas, made up of a mixture of other gases. About 78% is nitrogen, 21% oxygen and the rest other gases including carbon dioxide. It is invisible and has no smell. It can be felt and contained; it occupies space and has weight. It exerts pressure, pushing in all directions.

2 A space from which all air has been extracted is called a vacuum.

3 Oxygen is essential for life. All living things require oxygen and most get this from the air. (Others, such as fish, use the oxygen in water, and a few, such as yeast, break down complex compounds containing oxygen.)

Activities and experiments

1 Demonstrate that air exists and that its effect can be seen:
a) Look at motion caused by moving air – windmills, sailing ships, leaves and twigs in motion, seed dispersal, musical instruments, etc.
b) Make a small pinhole in a balloon, Blow it up and feel the air coming out.
c) Blow up a balloon. Is it possible to flatten it without letting the air out?
d) Hold a plastic bottle under water. Squash it and watch air bubble out.
e) Show that air has weight. Set up the apparatus shown in the diagram. First hang two empty balloons on each end and balance the dowel exactly. With a felt pen, mark where one pair are hung. Take them off and blow them up before replacing them. The blown up balloons will tilt the dowel.

2 Show that air takes up room:
a) If a funnel with a narrow stem is put into a bottle and the space round it is sealed with plasticine, the children can see what happens when they try to pour water into the bottle. The water will either stay in the funnel – because there is no room in the bottle – or will go in in spurts, with the air bubbling out – because there is only room for the water if some of the air can escape.
   If the plasticine is taken away, the water can run freely. Why?
b) If a jar is inverted and pushed into water (a small aquarium is useful for these experiments) the water will rise so far, but will not fill the jar. The air can be compressed, but it still occupies space and the water cannot get in. If a dry tissue is put in the bottom of the jar before it is inverted, the children can see that the jar can be pushed right under the water, but the tissue remains dry. Does it make any difference how deep the water is? What happens if the jar is tilted?

3 Children like the well-known experiment of sliding a card over the surface of a jar or tumbler completely full of water, and then inverting it. This needs to be done smoothly (a jerk will dislodge the card). Air pressure holds the card on and the water does not spill.

4 Suckers stay on a wall because the air is squeezed out as they are pushed on to the wall. The air pushing on the outside holds the sucker firmly fixed. If a sucker with a hole in it is used, the experiment will not work.

5 A simple syringe can be used to draw up water. As the plunger is pulled upwards, the air pressure inside is reduced and water flows into the barrel because the outside air pushes down on the surface of the water. Can the children suck water into a plastic bottle in the same way?

6 If the children keep small mammals or budgerigars, a simple drinker can be made for them (see diagram).

7 Show the effect of air resistance by making toy parachutes from material or thin paper (see diagram). Children can devise their own models.

8 Make flying toys such as paper darts and aeroplanes. Which fly the best? Talk about flight. How do air currents help birds? Older children can find out more about aircraft.

9 Further developments:
   a) Air as a supporter of burning and respiration
   b) Wind and wind scales
   c) The story of flight

Useful apparatus

Plastic bottles and pots; plastic funnels; modelling clay; balloons; string; dowel; washing-up bowls or aquaria; fabric; thin paper; cartridge paper; cotton; washers; feathers; drinking straws; simple syringes

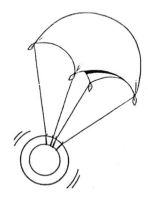

Making a parachute. Drop it from a window, or stand on a table and drop it

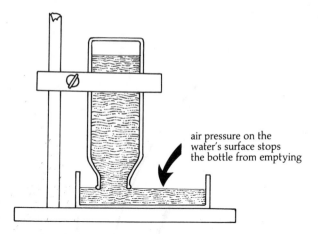

air pressure on the water's surface stops the bottle from emptying

A drinker for birds or small animals

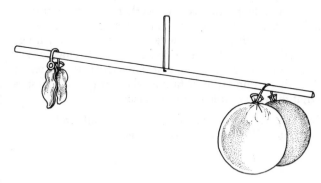

Showing that air has weight. The rod must be carefully balanced before the balloons at one end are inflated

Weather is a topic familiar to all of us, and even the youngest children make observations about it. Keeping weather records is fairly common in schools, but it can be a routine and rather boring task. It becomes far more interesting if children can be shown how much weather affects them and their environment, and how all life on earth is dependent on rainfall.

General notes

1 Weather involves cloud, rainfall and humidity; sun and temperature; air pressure and winds. Conditions vary from season to season and place to place. The water cycle is a continuous process involving evaporation and condensation. A saucer of water will disappear gradually (more quickly in warm dry weather) because it has evaporated. It has become water vapour in the air. A mist of tiny droplets forms on a glass of very cold water if we breathe on it, or leave it outside for a while. The water vapour in the air has condensed, and changed back into droplets.

2 Rain water comes indirectly from the sea which occupies such a large area of the earth's surface that it is the source of most water evaporation. The water evaporates, forming vapour in the atmosphere. As this rises and cools, it condenses into droplets which form clouds. Moving air carries these clouds overland where further cooling results in the formation of larger drops. These fall to the earth as rain. Rain flows through the ground, gradually forming springs as it meets the impervious layers of rock, and these feed the streams and rivers which ultimately flow into the sea.

3 The water content of the soil varies according to the composition of the soil and the amount and depth of rock layers. Clay soils, composed of tiny particles, become waterlogged as the particles cling together. Soils containing humus absorb and retain water, but they also have plenty of air spaces. Water finds its own level with its surface forming a horizontal line. This happens in soil, the level being known as the 'water table'. Where a lake or pool is formed, the water table is above ground (the surface level of the pool). Marshes show that the water table is at ground level.

4 All plants and animals are dependent on rainfall, and without water all living organisms would die.

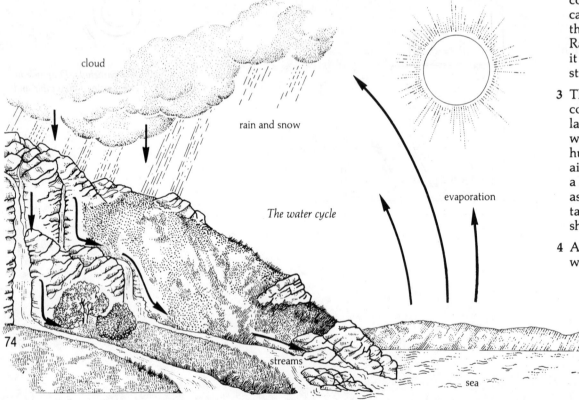

cloud

rain and snow

The water cycle

evaporation

streams

sea

5 Waterproofing is important if plants and animals, including humans, are to withstand rain. Skin and feathers are naturally waterproof, while leaves and bark absorb little water. People need to waterproof their home, to wear waterproof clothing in the rain, and to protect such things as wood and metal from the wet.

Activities and experiments

1 Find out something about rainfall. Are some places wetter than others? How much rain falls in one week in a given place? Make simple rain gauges. These can be used for comparison and need not be calibrated accurately.

2 Look at waterproof clothing and devise tests to see if they really are waterproof.

3 Various materials can be collected to test if they are waterproof. These can be cut so that they will go over the top of, say, an empty food tin (with the top removed with a rotary cutter) and fixed with a rubber band. All the prepared tins can then be watered with a watering can with a rose. The children can then see which materials have let the least water through. Test polythene, rubber sheeting, metal foil, loosely woven cotton material, firmly woven cotton, nylon, denim, gaberdine, knitted wool, paper, etc. Experiment to see if material that is stretched tightly is more waterproof than material left loose (show the children an umbrella).

4 Collect together building materials such as bricks, tiles and slates. If a brick is placed in a bowl of water, it will absorb a great deal of the water, and children can see this. They can be shown the damp course of the school building or a house, and can try to see how water is prevented from rising up a house wall. If one brick is half immersed in water and another is put on top, the water will eventually rise through both of them. If the same experiment is repeated, but a sheet of roof felt or polythene is put in between, the top brick stays dry. Roofing materials can be looked at and discussed – tiles, slates, tarred felt, corrugated iron, plastic and thatch. Ways of treating wood so that it will not rot can be looked at. Children can experiment with oil, paint and creosote to see if these will waterproof wood.

5 Plant seeds in dry soil in pots and keep these outside. Protect some seeds from rain by covering them. What happens to the seeds?

6 Get a large box of completely dry sand or soil. This can be put outside on a wet day and the children can find out if the rain goes right through. Make sure that the box has a large enough surface for the surface water to drain off, and that the soil or sand is at least 20 cm deep.

7 Collect weather sayings, such as the following. Use these for discussion, and let the children find out if they are true:
St Swithin's Day, if it should rain,
For forty days it will remain.

Red sky at night; a shepherd's delight,
Red sky in the morning; a shepherd's warning.
(Does this mean rain?)

They can try to find out other weather sayings for themselves.

8 See section 19.

Useful apparatus

Washing-up liquid bottles; slates; tiles; bricks; roof felt; polythene sheeting; fabrics of various sorts; umbrellas; rubber sheeting; bottles and jars; watering can (with a rose); seeds; sand and soil; rubber bands

A rain gauge made from washing-up liquid bottles (this will not give an accurate measure of rainfall, but it can be used for comparison)

—top of bottle

—base of bottle

Children already know something about the sun. They know it does not shine at night or when it is cloudy. They may not realize that night and day depend on the position of the earth in relation to the sun, and that it is the source of light even when not visible. The growth of plants depends on the sun since photosynthesis can only take place in the presence of light.

Summer days are warmer, and children can see this by the clothes they wear, plant growth, animal activity and the fact that heating in homes and schools is no longer necessary.

General notes

1 As the earth travels around the sun each year, it spins on its own axis, and it is the tilt of this axis that governs our seasons. At different times of the year, different parts of the earth are tilted towards the sun. Britain is at its closest to the sun in June. In December it is at its furthest from the sun. The days are shorter, the nights longer, and any sunshine is weak.

2 Plants and animals adapt themselves to the changing seasons. In summer, plants are in full leaf and are building up reserves of food for winter. They are flowering and producing seed, and those which grow very rapidly produce several generations during the summer months (e.g. Shepherd's Purse).

With plentiful vegetation, animals can feed well during the summer, and conditions are favourable for breeding. The hair and fur of most animals is less thick than in winter, and there may be obvious colour changes.

The life cycles of many insects are fairly short in warm weather when food is easy to obtain, e.g. houseflies, many butterflies, ladybirds and bees are active.

3 Shadows give an indication of the position of the sun in the sky. When the sun is low, the shadows will be long, and when it is overhead at mid-day, they will be short and clearly outlined.

Note Children should be told never to look directly at the sun.

4 When the weather is warm and the air is not humid, washing will dry in a very short time because the water in it evaporates quickly. Water will also evaporate from ponds and pools, and water left in flat dishes soon disappears. In time of prolonged drought, there is considerable danger to wildlife in ponds and streams, and plants with short roots which only penetrate the surface layers will die unless they are watered.

5 Plants rely on sunlight to manufacture their food. Using light energy, the water taken in by the roots and the carbon dioxide taken in by the leaves are built up into complex substances. Without light, plants will die. Children do not need to understand photosynthesis but they can see that all life on earth depends on plants either directly or indirectly; plant-eating animals feed on vegetation, and other animals feed on the plant eaters.

6 For children who like facts, tell them that the sun is a small star with a surface temperature of about 6000°C. It is 150 million km from earth.

Activities and experiments

1 Make a simple shadow clock (see section 29).

2 Investigate shadows. The youngest children can look at the shapes, can try to run away from their own shadows, can draw round them and can make shadow patterns. Older

children can find out how the sun's position alters a shadow, and how the light source causes variations in intensity. They can also find out more about temperature in sun and shade. This can be done by using thermometers, by melting fat, or by warming water in a shallow dish in the sun.

3 Some simple experiments can be done to show how plants need light.
   a) Plant mustard seeds in two pots, Keep both watered but put one in a cupboard in the dark and put the other in a light place. The children can see what happens to the plants as they grow. Those in the dark will grow long and spindly, with yellow leaves (etiolation) and die after a time. Those in the light will be green and healthy.
   b) Well-established plants can be placed on a window sill and left unturned. All the leaves will grow towards the light. If a plant such as a geranium is used, it can be seen that the leaves will position themselves so that they get the maximum light.

4 Look at the indications of summer or the approach of warmer weather in plants and animals:
   a) Plants – rapid germination of seeds; growth of vegetation generally; flowers; insects visiting flowers; other insects feeding on plants (aphids, caterpillars, etc.); fruit ripening.
   b) Animals – loss of thicker fur or hair (dogs, cats, sheep); more animals seen around; people wear less clothing.

5 Devise experiments to show the speed of evaporation of water on hot or sunny days. Discuss the importance of this, for example, as part of the water cycle (see section 34).

6 People wear sunglasses in the summer. Children can wear sunglasses to see if things look different with tinted glass. They can look at bright things – a white wall, shiny metal – in sunlight and see if it is easier to look at them wearing the

glasses. (Again, stress the importance of not looking directly at the sun.) The power of the sun's rays can be demonstrated using a magnifying glass to focus the rays onto a piece of paper. The children will see the paper burn. Although this is not an experiment young children should be encouraged to try, it can be used to show one of the dangers of leaving bottles about. The curved surface of the bottle acts in the same way as the magnifying glass, and heath and hedgerow fires can be started very easily if bottles or broken glass are left about in the countryside.

Useful apparatus

Flowerpots; soil; seeds; sunglasses; tinted acetate; growing plants (in pots); garden canes; chalk; large sheets of paper; thermometers (outdoor and soil); magnifying glass; camera; flat dishes; cooking fat

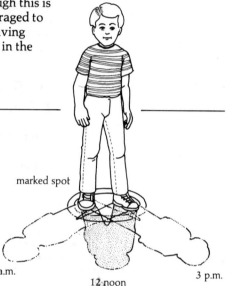

marked spot

9 a.m. 12 noon 3 p.m.

Moving shadows

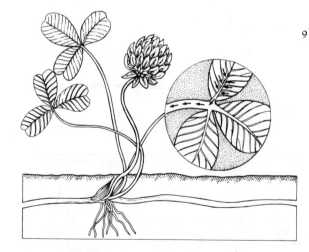

Plants need the energy in sunlight to make food

77

It may be uncomfortable to be cold, and living permanently in a cold climate means that plants and animals have to adapt for survival at very low temperatures. There are some advantages in being able to freeze substances, however. The one within the easy understanding of children is refrigeration of foodstuffs, both as a preservative and as a means of making such things as ice cream and ice lollies.

General notes

1 Temperature is measured in degrees – normally in either centigrade or fahrenheit. These are, quite simply, two different scales. On the centigrade scale, water boils at 100° and freezes at 0°. On the fahrenheit scale, it boils at 212° and freezes at 32°.

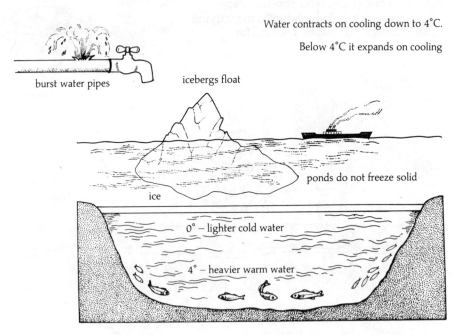

Water contracts on cooling down to 4°C.

Below 4°C it expands on cooling

burst water pipes

icebergs float

ice

ponds do not freeze solid

0° – lighter cold water

4° – heavier warm water

2 When water is changed to ice, it expands. A given volume of ice is therefore lighter than the same volume of water. Burst pipes are caused by expanding ice, but it is only when the ice thaws that the bursts become obvious.

3 It is only in exceptionally cold weather that the water in a pond will freeze completely. The water begins to expand as it cools below 4°C. It is then lighter than the slightly warmer water found deeper in the pond. The surface then freezes, leaving the water at the bottom ice free. This protects water animals.

4 To counteract cold, animals develop thicker coats, burrow underground, hibernate or migrate. People wear insulating clothes to keep in the body heat.

5 Food can be preserved for long periods by freezing because the bacteria causing decay cannot reproduce under very cold conditions, even though they are not killed. A refrigerator keeps food cool, and so keeps it fresh for short periods. Completely frozen food will stay fresh for a very long time.

6 When a liquid evaporates, it takes heat from its surroundings, thus cooling them. The usual refrigerating liquid contains ammonia because it absorbs heat well when it liquefies. Anti-freeze mixtures, used in car radiators, contain liquids which freeze at lower temperatures than 0°C.

7 Hailstones are frozen raindrops. Snowflakes are made up of crystals of ice formed from frozen water vapour. Frost is frozen dew and condensed vapour. Icicles form when snow or ice starts to melt and then refreezes.

Activities and experiments

1 Look at the activities of animals in winter:
  a) Hibernation – some animals hibernate completely (frog, snail) but others will come out for food during finer weather (squirrel)
  b) Growth of thicker hair or fur
  c) Building of shelters and homes (including humans)

2 Look at survival in the extreme cold of the arctic and antarctic. Find out how polar bears, penguins and seals survive. What about people?

3 Find out about ice. Fill different plastic pots and bottles with water and put them outside in cold weather or in a refrigerator. Note how the ice formed rises above the level of the containers. What will happen to a bottle of milk? To show how pipes will burst, fill a thin plastic bottle with water and screw the lid on firmly. Leave this to freeze. The bottle will usually split.

4 When it snows, take the opportunity to look at the symmetry of snowflakes. Let the snowflakes fall on a very cold sheet of glass or perspex. If looked at quickly, with a strong hand lens or microscope, the symmetrical patterns can be seen.

5 Food preservation by freezing makes an interesting topic. First carry out some tests on such things as bread, milk and stewed fruit. Put one portion of each in a freezer, one each in the refrigerator and leave one each in the classroom. Note what happens after one or two weeks. Find out which foods can be frozen. Make a collection of frozen food packets and use these for a display about freezing and food preparation.

6 Make ice cream or ice lollies. If a refrigerator is readily available, the children can try out recipes of their own.

7 Try freezing different liquids. Will they all freeze in the temperatures available? Try cooking oil, washing-up liquid, tea, milk, etc.

8 Break up some ice into small pieces and take the temperature. Mix in salt and take the temperature again. Salty water freezes at a temperature lower than 0°C, so why is salt put on footpaths in icy conditions? Find out why ice is slippery and why you can skate on it. (Ice will melt slightly under pressure, and refreeze when the pressure is removed.)

Useful apparatus

Thermometers (large and clearly marked); plastic bottles and pots; frozen food packets; pictures of arctic animals; strong hand lens or simple binocular microscope; milk bottle; perspex or glass sheet

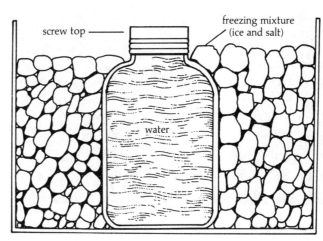

As water freezes it will expand and crack the jar

A thermometer

79

If you stand on high ground and look around at the countryside, you can see the patchwork of fields. Most fields will be separated by hedges which are still so plentiful that they form valuable nature reserves; but as fields get larger and larger, hedges are being uprooted. With them goes a wide variety of wildlife. They are so interesting, both historically and biologically, that it will be a great pity if we do not do our best to conserve these rich natural habitats.

It is because of the abundance of hedgerows that our natural woodland birds are able to survive in agricultural areas, and even newer park and garden hedges can provide cover and nesting sites for the more familiar birds. Each hedge has its own ecology – depending largely on its age and position – and this is well worth studying, because of the plant and animal life that abounds.

Because of its wide base the 'A' shaped hedge tends to be better cover for wildlife

General notes

1 Hedges can be field, road, parish or garden boundaries, ornamental features or windbreaks. The parish boundary hedges are likely to be the oldest, and these can often be found marked on old maps. (Use the local library to find these.) Some idea of age can be ascertained by looking at the shrubs growing in the hedge. Although this must vary to some extent according to the way in which the hedge has been maintained and the type of soil in which it is planted, the number of different shrubs growing in a 30 m length is reasonably indicative of age.

In general a hedge that is about 100 years old will have only one or two species of shrub in a length, a 200 year old hedge will have two or three, and so on.

2 The number of nests found will depend on the way in which the hedge has been cared for, the number of shrubs present and the site.

The wildlife of the hedge will be influenced by the areas on either side of it, and the amount of plant growth in the immediate vicinity. For example, a hedge separating a woodland area from a field, with numerous plants growing underneath it, is much more likely to be rich in animal life than the hedge separating field from roadside where the verge is kept cut short, and there is considerable pollution by motor traffic.

3 The shrubs of the hedge are likely to be among the following: ash, beech, blackthorn, elder, elm, hawthorn, hazel, holly, privet, oak, sycamore and willow. It is also likely that you will be able to find crab apple, rose, yew and box. Hedges of various ornamental shrubs will be found in parks and gardens.

4 Plants growing under and in the hedge will vary according to districts but children will be able to find grasses, bramble, hogweed, bryony, ivy, campion, dandelion, vetch, cleavers, burdock, dock, etc. Ferns may be growing in some hedges, and less common plants such as cuckoo pint and primrose may be found.

5 Animal life can include caterpillars of various butterflies and moths, beetles, spiders, snails, harvestmen, bees, frogs and toads. Other visitors may be field mice, voles, hedgehogs, grasshoppers, rabbits, lizards and birds nesting in the hedge or feeding on the plant seeds and insects.

Activities and experiments

1 Most of the work will be field work for any project on hedges. The teacher should try to visit any likely hedge before taking the children there in order to plan the work. Prepare the children for the visit and make it clear what they can collect and what they must leave alone.
  a) Collect samples of litter (debris under the hedge)
  b) Collect leaves of plant species found. Collect samples of common flowers, but do not uproot
  c) Take note of any animal life seen

Older children can have a project sheet to work on, and most identification can be done back in the classroom.

2 Make a study of hedges in the district. How are these maintained? What is the purpose of each hedge?

3 Some town schools may not be able to make more than one visit to a hedge, but this will serve as a starter for further work. Children can find out about the history of hedges and may be able to find the remains of an old farm hedge in the most unlikely place. (Three or more very old hawthorns in a line usually indicate old farm land, and these can be seen even in built up areas.)

4 If possible, look at a stretch of hedge over a year and note the changes found. Use drawings and photographs to record these.

Useful apparatus

Camera; hand lenses; plastic bags and boxes; wax crayons; tape measures; small trowel; books for helping with identification

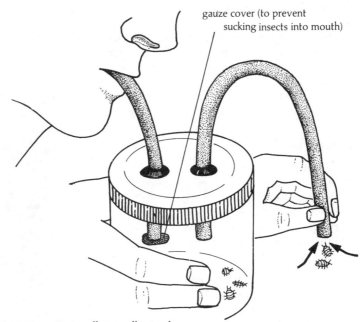

gauze cover (to prevent sucking insects into mouth)

Use a pooter to collect small animals

Children respond to, and learn from, their surroundings and should be given opportunities to explore beyond the classroom. There cannot be a set list of things that they should see and do – so much depends on the environment and the needs of the children – but their curiosity about their immediate world can be exploited and used to their benefit.

Any project which gives them the chance to make discoveries for themselves must be planned to suit individual needs, and should aim to sharpen their perception and give them practice in thinking about their surroundings in terms of space, size and number. As they get older, their attention can be concentrated on particular objects or themes which interest them.

The countryside, as we know it, is no longer very natural, but it supports a great deal of wildlife and genuinely wild places, with their own special characteristics, ought to be preserved. It is important to make children aware of what is around them and to encourage them to look at what is worth conserving.

General notes

1 Very little of our landscape is natural. Most has been made by people over thousands of years. Each area is, however, dependent on its own natural structure – rock, rivers, hills and mountains, moorland, shore and cliff.

2 There are many factors that have brought about changes in land patterns – earth movements, weathering, glacial and water erosion, etc., and the changes made by people continue to alter the environment. These changes include the spread of towns and roadways, newer farming methods, tourism, change in land use.

3 Children can collect information about the special features of different areas by many different means:
a) Use of children's holiday experiences
b) Collect photographs from them and their families
c) Make use of film, slides and television programmes
d) Undertake specialized studies such as birds of the coast and shore, woodland fungi, mammals in towns, and keep this information so that it can be used to build up detailed pictures of particular habitats
e) Use the school area for detailed study (see section 39) and exchange information with schools in other areas

Even in a town environment, many examples of wildlife can be found

4 Plants and animals vary considerably according to the environment. For example, sea birds are not normally found far from the coast. (An interesting topic, however, would be to look at the way in which gulls have adapted to life inland.) Even domestic animals vary. The fleece of downland sheep such as Southdown, differs from that of moorland and mountain sheep, such as Swaledale.

Activities and experiments

1 Decide on all the possible types of environment that the children are likely to know, and then plan to study one or more of these in some detail.

  The town environment – inner city and urban
  Agricultural environment – grassland, woodland, village
  Cliffs, shores, coastlines and estuaries
  Streams, rivers and ponds
  Moorland and heathland
  Mountains, hills and fells
  Forests and woods
  Roadways – including motorways, roads, paths and
  tracks

Use the project sheet at the end of the book for the initial study.

2 Choose any particular area (not too big) and find out as much as possible about its use, its history and any changes brought about in the last few years. Decide what effect this has had on the plant and animal life of the area. Example: widening of the road passing the school. To do this a hedge has been removed and a small pond filled in. The pond used to be a breeding place for frogs, and the hedge always had nests in it. Therefore, wildlife has been lost. In contrast, this road has taken big lorries off another small road where old trees were being damaged.

3 Younger children could undertake more limited studies. One is to look at paths, tracks and trails and find out whether they have been built or have been made by continual use (the tracks of children or animals across a field or waste land). They could also look at very specific environments:

  The school garden or the local park
  A farm
  A pond or pool
  A field or small wood

4 Plan an information exchange with schools in completely different areas so that each can build up a picture of, say, the plants and animals found around them.

Useful apparatus

Local maps; cameras; slides and film strips; boards and pencils for outdoor work; reference books for indoor work; portable tape recorder; measuring tapes; modelling clay (for model making)

The countryside, as we know it has been largely created by humans

Every school, no matter where it is situated, is in an environment which can provide suitable science topics. Although some schools have the obvious advantages of access to fields, forest, moorland, hills or the seashore, even the school built in the middle of an industrial city has a world to be explored. It is almost impossible to separate environmental biology from environmental history and geography, and the suggestions made can include any, or all, of these.

Children like discovering things for themselves, but preparation is still needed. The teacher needs to know exactly what his or her area has to offer and needs to plan for the children's likely requirements. It must be appreciated that the environment can include the school – both inside and outside – and that some of the work can be done when the weather is too bad for outdoor excursions.

General notes

1 If asked to describe a house, children will almost certainly mention windows, doors and chimneys but will be unlikely to note the lichen on the brickwork or the signs of wear and deterioration. Encourage them to look at such features as:

    Building materials and features of buildings
    Streets and road names, and street furniture
    Railway lines, canals, rivers, streams
    Walls and hedges
    Industrial features
    Villages, farms, signs of settlement
    Fields, crops, domestic animals, farms
    Prehistoric and historic sites
    Plant and animal life
    Geological features, rocks, cliffs
    Lakes, ponds, seashore
    Specific sites – harbours, quarries, lighthouses, factories, parks and gardens

2 Always plan visits, however simple they may seem. If the visit is to a museum or castle, it is worth talking to the curator or education officer first.

Activities and experiments

1 Make a general survey of the area before you begin other work. See section 38 and use the Project sheet at the end of the book, if you are working with older children. Younger ones can talk about what they have seen and can make up a composite picture or frieze showing the main features of the area. After this, decide what each child or group is going to look at in detail.

2 For winter work, use the school as the actual basis for the topic:
  a) Shapes, stresses and strains
    Windows, doors and other openings
    Materials – brick, concrete, glass, wood, plastic, metals, paint, paper
  b) Heating and lighting
  c) Roofs and waterproofing, damp courses, pipes and drains
    Walls and brickwork
  d) Services going into the school – water, gas, electricity
  e) Playgrounds – plants and animals associated with the playground (trees, weeds such as dandelion and willow-herb, mosses and lichens)

3 Outside the school the children could look at:
    Trees
    Streets, roads and lanes, other trackways
    Bridges, fences and walls, gates
    Ponds, pools, streams, canals
    Waste land, gardens, parks, hedges, fields
    Old buildings, churches and churchyards

4 Look at walls (see section 40).

5 Look at walks, paths and trackways and ask the following questions:
  a) How old is it?
  b) Is it a deliberately made trackway or has it appeared because of constant usage?
  c) Are there any trees? Are they growing naturally or have they been cut or lopped?
  d) Are there any signs of pollution?
  e) Make plant charts of the trackway, marking in all the plants found. Are there many different types of plants? Were they planted or did they get there naturally?
  f) Are there any signs of animal life? What are these?

6 Investigate the habitats of plants and animals in the area. How are these affected by roads, buildings, agricultural work, etc.?

7 Look at edges and verges: country roads offer more scope for investigation than town streets, but both can pose some problems for the children to solve. What effect does cutting have on grass verges? Does it destroy any natural habitats? Does traffic pollution affect plant growth? How well are any trees growing? Has anything affected their growth (lopping, damage from vehicles that have hit them or rubbed them, nails driven into them for various reasons, growing against or near a wall or fence)? What are the commonest plants?

Useful apparatus

Tape measures and rulers; camera; collecting bags and boxes; local maps; tape recorder; local guidebooks

Common brick bonds

uncoursed squared rubble – 'cocks and hens' stone coping

stretcher bond

English bond (the strongest)

Sussex bond

Flemish bond

Wherever the school is situated, and whatever the type of environment, there are always walls to be found. They may be the very old walls of a Norman castle or they may be found on a newly built housing estate, but the way they are built, their purposes, their history and any living organisms connected with them will provide the basis for an investigation by children. Because of the proximity of walls of all types, they make a suitable study for any class at any time of the year. They are a useful link between several study areas – science (natural history, structure, type of stone used), history (age, style, purpose), mathematics (size, shape, strength, tessellation).

Old walls are probably the most interesting, but any wall can be used to show children that there is always something interesting to be found if only they will look around them and think about what they see.

General notes

1 Some walls are built of natural stone. These may be coursed (laid in regular layers), uncoursed (built of irregular blocks), pointed with mortar or cement, or they may have small pebbles between the larger stones. Natural stone tends to be used in the districts where the stones are found, e.g. Cotswold limestone, Cornish slate. Stone has been used for building since ancient times. It was first used in the parts of the country where stone was easily available – Wiltshire and Yorkshire, for example.

2 Natural stone walls were also built as field boundaries – usually stone and earth walls, slate walls or dry stone walls. Dry stone walls are built without mortar and are made up of rocks and stones fitted together to make very strong and stable structures. These walls are common in the north and west, but rare in the south, and unfortunately, many are disappearing as they are torn down to enlarge fields. Most dry stone walls are wider at the base, and the stones are chosen and placed with care so that there are very few gaps.

3 The use of evenly sized bricks for building walls is much quicker, and the patterns formed by the bricklaying are called bonds. Different brick bonds can be seen on different buildings. The herringbone pattern is a rare one, though sometimes found in very old walls. There is one such at Tamworth Castle in Staffordshire.

4 Walls, old or new, have many uses:
Houses, churches, castles and other fortifications
Town walls, field boundaries, garden and park walls
Dams, harbour walls and retaining walls
Barns, stores, factories and many other buildings

All or any of these may support special features such as date and name stones; carvings and ornament; stiles, gates, arches, doors and holes; sundials; straighteners.

Activities and experiments

1 Look at walls in the area of the school or in places that the children can visit. Decide what sort of work young children could do.
Have the walls any historical significance?
Are the walls part of buildings?
Are they decorative of just functional?
Are the walls boundaries of some sort?
Of what material are they built?
Have they any interesting features?
Are there any plants growing on or alongside them?
Are there any animals connected with the walls?

2 Plan a visit to a site where children can look at a wall. Take photographs of it and let them make rubbings. Use thin strong paper and thick black wax crayons. Brick walls make extremely good rubbings, and the brick bonds show up well.

Look at the natural history of the wall:
a) Plants growing on the wall; roots between the stones and in crevices, e.g. ivy-leaved toadflax, stonecrop, mosses, lichens, ferns
b) Plants climbing the wall but with their roots in the ground, e.g. ivy
c) Plants growing at the base of a wall, e.g. grasses, dock, nettles, dandelion, vetch, bramble
d) Animals found on the wall and among the stones, e.g. snails, spiders, woodlice, ants, earwigs
e) Animals seen on and near walls, e.g. field mice, birds (sparrows, starlings, robins, wagtails, pigeons; some of the owls will nest on ledges of ruined buildings)

3 Get the children to work in groups on specific topics connected with the chosen wall:
a) History (even a new wall has a history)
b) Structure – material used; building; pattern; method of holding the stone together; height; thickness
c) Structural details – holes; gates and stiles; name plates and signs; ornamentation
d) Natural history – plants and animals found on the wall and at the base
e) Signs of wear, tear and erosion – has any part fallen or been replaced? Signs of pollution; damage

4 Look at building materials, both natural and manufactured. Test these for strength and durability. Try building a dry stone wall or a brick wall. Build model walls. Make a collection of bricks and stones.

Useful apparatus

Cement; sand; clay; modelling clay; black wax crayons; camera; boxes for collections; tape measures; tape recorder; hand lenses

Building a wall – a template can be used to keep the correct shape, but many wallers work by eye

Not all children live near or have the opportunity to visit the seaside, but they ought to be aware of the variety of living things associated with the shore line. Even a school trip lasting only a few hours can start off some interesting work, but it is far better if the children can spend some time exploring this environment and discovering for themselves some of the plants and animals found here.

Regrettably, much of the natural beauty of many beaches is being destroyed by the quantity of plastic rubbish that is constantly being washed ashore and, much more seriously, by oil. This is not only dirty and unsightly but also causes the death of thousands of sea birds each year, and destroys many other animals and plants. Children should know about this and see the results for themselves because they may in the future be able to help with the conservation of some of the very varied coastal areas found round this country.

Cliff features

headland
arch
cliff
cave
stack
rock pool
rocks and boulders
(rounded by wave action)
beach (resting on a wave-cut platform)

General notes

1 The shore is affected by tides. When arranging a visit, you will need to know the times of high tides both from a safety angle and to ascertain when the maximum amount of beach is uncovered.

2 Rocky shores are probably the most interesting. It is almost impossible to list all the plants and animals that may be seen, so a good reference book is essential. Some of the following will be found:

Sea anenomes – animals which feed on other water organisms
Crustaceans – crabs, shrimps, hermit crabs and barnacles
Molluscs – limpets, periwinkles, topshells and whelks
Tube worms – seen as white growths on rocks and shells
Fish
Starfish (echinoderms)
Sea weeds – plants adapted to life in the sea; many species
Sea birds

3 The shore may be sandy, shingle or rocky. Each is a quite different habitat. The boundary of the shore may be marked by dunes, cliffs or rocky slopes. Each area supports its own plant life.

Activities and experiments

1 Make detailed studies of a particular area – rock pool, sand dune, a shingle beach, the shore between high and low tide marks, the strand line, a cliff.

2 Look at birds and other animals found at the seashore.

3 The children can collect shells in plastic bags or buckets but use plastic boxes for very small fragile shells. Back at school, the shells should be soaked in a weak solution of household

bleach for 24 hours, rinsed in clean water and left to dry. The shells can be stored in shallow cardboard boxes. If they are identified, the shell and the name label can be stuck into the box and the whole display covered with clingfilm.

4 Unless the school has a seawater aquarium live specimens should be put into a bucket for a short time so that they can be looked at and then returned to the sea (or wherever found).

5 Interesting items can be kept and labelled – skate or dogfish egg cases (mermaid's purse), dried seaweeds, driftwood, pebbles, bones, fossils, crab shells, feathers. Some driftwood may show signs of shipworm attack.

6 It is possible to press examples of some of the smaller seaweeds. Do not try to preserve more than a small specimen. Wash the weeds in clean water, lay the sample on thick damp drawing paper and leave to dry out for a few hours. Cover with a piece of waxed paper (the inner bag from a cornflakes packet will do very well), then several layers of newspaper. Put a board and something heavy on the top and leave for several weeks. Specimens can then be mounted as wanted. They look best if put onto thick card and covered with adhesive plastic film.

7 Start with photographs of the site visited and add models, drawings and paintings made by the children. Show the specimens suitably mounted or displayed – a tray of sand makes a good base for shells and stones. Charts showing such things as the movement of periwinkles, bird counts (see section 20) and profiles of rock pools will add to the interest. Label everything and add a taped commentary explaining the area and the work done. A slide projector with slides of seashore plants and animals can be put out for visitors to use.

8 Further developments:
a) Life in the sea
b) Other animals that live in shells
c) A closer look at the rocks of the coast
d) Setting up a marine aquarium
e) Looking at estuaries
f) Seasonal change

Useful apparatus

Plastic bags and boxes; buckets; nets; binoculars; camera; spades; tape measures; hand lenses

Seaweeds are flowerless plants. They all contain chlorophyll but the green is sometimes masked by brown or red

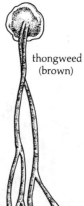

thongweed (brown)

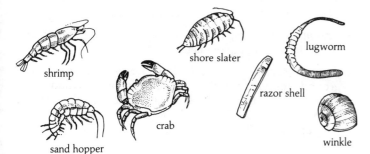

shrimp

shore slater

lugworm

sand hopper

crab

razor shell

winkle

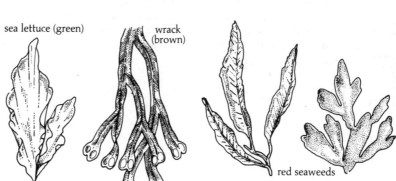

sea lettuce (green)

wrack (brown)

red seaweeds

89

The natural history of the countryside is an obvious subject for study, but looking at the ecology of town wildlife can be both practical and rewarding. The word 'ecology' comes from two Greek words – *oikos* meaning homes and *logos* meaning the study of. So it is the study of plant and animal life in their own environment.

This environment may be an unlikely industrial town or city, but many plants and animals are able to live here successfully and have established themselves so well that they have become a part of the town's profile. Sometimes traces of old habitats can be found – parkland that is the remaining part of a natural forest, remnants of old hedges, vestigial river shores, old trees, old gardens. It is often possible to trace original agricultural or village life from street names in city centres. Look for such names as Orchard Street, Mill Lane, Green Lane, Far Fold and Woodland Croft.

General notes

1 A study of the natural history of a town, whether inner city or suburb, should not be just a survey of the plants and animals, but a study of the ways in which these have adapted to life there. The complex environment of the town has been created by people, but it is diverse and supports a great deal of wildlife, much of which has become a part of the surroundings. For example, the rosebay willow-herb was uncommon 100 years ago, but has flourished since the 1940s when it colonised bombsites and is now the commonest town plant. Elephant hawk-moth larvae feed on rosebay, and so now these are also found in towns.

Some plants grow in unusual places (gutters, cracks in walls and pavements etc)

2 Buildings resemble the rocks of cliffs and mountains in some ways, so mosses will establish themselves on buildings in time. Mosses hold water and tend to collect debris which gradually forms a growing base for such plants as grasses, ragwort and dandelion. Birds which roost on rocks in their original natural state, will nest and roost on the ledges of buildings (starling, pigeon, wagtail).

Gardens, sports grounds and parks provide imitations of woodland and pasture land, and trees can also be found in streets. There may be reservoirs and canals providing aquatic habitats, and schools may have grounds with plants growing in them. These plants will shelter a host of small animals.

Activities and experiments

1 Make a survey of any open space within a city – park, garden, churchyard, playing field, canal bank, wasteland. Which plants have established themselves naturally and which have been introduced? (Younger children can make simple plant counts.) The Project sheet at the end of the book can be used.

2 Look at the effects of pollution – dirt and grime, sooty coating on leaves, dead and dying plants, etc. Lichens are affected by sulphurous gases in the air, so look for lichens on trees and walls. What does their absence indicate?

3 Find plants growing in unusual places such as guttering and cracks in walls and pavements.

4 Create a piece of wasteland. Either dig over an area of ground removing any signs of plant life, or put wooden boxes of soil in the playground. Leave these alone and watch them over the year. Which plants grow? Discuss how this has happened. Chart the time factor.

5 Make a tree survey. Trees can be found in parks, gardens, school grounds, churchyards and along walks and streets. The plane is a common town tree. It has managed to survive dirty and smoky conditions because its bark continuously peels off, getting rid of the accumulated dirt, and its leaves tend to repel dust and grime. Lime and sycamore also grow well in a town, as do beech, birch, laburnum, maple and hawthorn. Evergreens are not suitable because they keep their leaves and accumulations of dirt build up on them to such an extent that the trees are unable to breathe or absorb light energy.

6 The mammals of towns can be wild or domestic. Try to find out which live in your town. Do any of them cause any nuisance? How serious is this? How is it dealt with? (Look at rats, foxes and dogs, for example.)

7 Make a similar study of birds. Sparrows, pigeons and starlings are the commonest, but gulls will be seen round rubbish tips and many other birds are seen at times. Look at the problem of starlings coming into towns to roost at night.

8 Look at the ways in which plants and animals have adapted, and at the species of trees that can survive pollution and damage. Look at the ways in which authorities care for parks, streets, etc.

Useful apparatus

Camera; tape measures; hand lenses; trundle wheel; boxes and bags: trowels; bird table; local maps; tape recorder (for talking to local people)

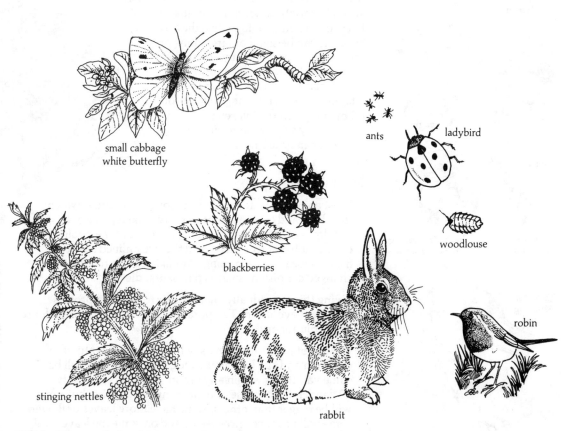

small cabbage white butterfly

ants   ladybird

blackberries

woodlouse

stinging nettles

rabbit

robin

Which of these can be found in your town?

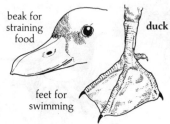

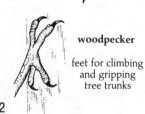

beak for
catching
fish

heron

feet for
grasping
and tearing

beak for
tearing
flesh

eagle

parrot

feet for
perching

beak for breaking
nuts and seeds

beak for
straining
food

duck

feet for
swimming

woodpecker

feet for climbing
and gripping
tree trunks

92

Even though children may look at many examples of plants
and animals, it may be some time before they realize
the wide variations within a familiar group.
They all recognize a dog when they see one,
but dogs can be small or large, long or
short haired, and of many colours.
A great deal of the science concerned
with variation in living things and
adaptation of living things (evolution)
is beyond primary children but,
treated very simply, some interesting
material can be learned.

General notes

1 Most animals are adapted to the conditions under which
they live, and these adaptations have taken place over
hundreds of years. For example, the neck of the giraffe
enables it to eat tree leaves and the streamlined shape of
fishes is ideal for swimming. Animals unable to adapt to
changed conditions such as dinosaurs, die out.

2 Living things gradually change their forms by a process
known as evolution. Temporary changes, often seasonal, are
not evolutionary.

3 Groups of plants or animals will have certain features in
common and can be classified together, but there will be
some variations within any group. It is easy to identify
10 dandelions because of their many similarities, but some
will be bigger than others, some have more leaves or flowers,
some will produce fewer seeds, and on some the leaves will
vary in shape.

Activities and experiments

1 Search for collections of living things, such as birds on the school bird table. List the characteristics that they have in common. (Feathers, beaks, two legs, two wings, feet with divided toes, etc.) List the ways in which they vary. (Size, colour, shape of beak, food, way of flying, etc.)

2 Make this activity a little more difficult by looking at the guinea pigs. Here there are fewer visible variations, but they are still there.

3 Look at tree leaves and find out the many different shapes and sizes. Are all the leaves from one tree the same?

4 Children can look at themselves. Everyone in the class is human and approximately the same age. What have they in common? How do they differ?

5 Older children can work out the distribution of variation in some fairly simple examples: What is the average number of seeds in a pod of, say, broom? By how much does the size of leaves on one tree vary? (Work out approximate areas on squared paper.)

6 In any area you can visit, find ways in which plants and animals have apparently adapted themselves to life there. Some examples are:
Earthworm living in soil (look at shape, food, method of feeding)
Limpet living on rocks beaten by the sea
Gulls now living in urban areas
Birds' beaks in relation to the food eaten
Bramble climbing in a hedge

7 Make a study of seasonal adaptations: leaf fall. Why? Plants dying down. Seeds lying dormant. Migration and hibernation. Change of colour or thickness of coat.

8 Look at other adaptations, such as frogs changing colours according to habitat; ability of plants to climb and cling.

Useful apparatus

Camera; books; pictures; slides; hand lenses; collecting bags; trays; writing boards
Note The children could record their findings on charts such as those shown here. The handwriting demonstrates how data might be entered.

penguin

flightless bird; wings have become swimming flippers

lung-fish

with lungs as well as gills they can withstand drought

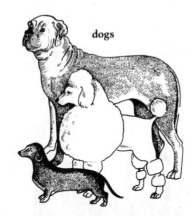

dogs

selective breeding has produced many variations of one species

zebra - *camouflage*

93

Very few natural areas remain. The countryside, once covered with oak forests, is largely unforested as the result of the cultivation of food. There is also less of it as towns and industrial areas have grown so much.

Accepting this, it is still important to conserve the open spaces, the plant and animal life and the variety of environments that do exist. It is equally important that these are not destroyed by pollution – the contamination of land and water by industrial waste, traffic, rubbish, dust, oil, chemicals including herbicides and pesticides, and acid rain.

General notes

1 Change in the use of the land does not necessarily mean that plants and animals are killed, because many will adapt to a new environment. Change caused by pollution, however, can alter the balance of life to such an extent that many species are affected.

Herbicide sprayed on vegetation → → → eaten by snails → → → eaten by birds which may die or be unable to breed successfully.

2 If children are to be taught about conservation, they must learn how to collect and study specimens without causing harm.
a) Never damage trees in any way.
b) Never pull plants out of the ground.
c) Collect one flower only. Any rare plants should be looked at and then left alone.
d) Put back any stones, rocks or logs which have been moved in exactly the same place. Every stone may conceal a mini-environment, and careless collecting may destroy it.
e) If frog spawn is being collected, take about 20 eggs only. This will be sufficient for classroom study. When the tadpoles have begun to change into frogs, return them to the pond again.
f) Never disturb nesting birds and never take eggs from nests. In many cases, the birds are protected and it is illegal to take eggs.
g) Do not kill insects when collecting them. It is far better to study them alive.

Activities and experiments

1 Look at the effects of pollution in any area near the school. Examples:
a) Streams, river and pools – look for clean water, healthy water plants and many small animals (water shrimps, insect larvae); bank plants growing freely; absence of rubbish.
b) Hedges and coppices – look for bushes with healthy leaves and flowers; look for insect life and visiting birds: see how the hedge is maintained.
c) Woodland, parkland and trees – look at the trees. Is the bark free from soot and damage? Are there any algae on the trunks? (Lichens die in air polluted by sulphur dioxide.) Rub the leaves with a clean tissue to see how dirty it becomes; look for dead and dying branches; look for signs of disease and damage.
d) Seashore – look for tar on the beach; look for rubbish and rotting vegetation; a healthy shore will have worm casts in the sand and many barnacles, whelks etc. on the rocks.

2 Very young children can look at pollution in terms of rubbish lying around (this could be done at school), damage to local trees, and wear and tear caused by people.

3 Plan a conservation scheme. This can involve a very small area or be a major project lasting a whole year and making use of local people and resources. Examples:
a) Rescue a piece of waste ground and turn it into a wild garden.
b) Clean up a part of the school playground and make a flower garden.

Many different gases released in to the atmosphere from various sources, such as factories, power stations and road vehicles, cause chemical changes in the atmosphere and acid rain to fall that devastates plant life and destroys stone buildings

c) Make a study of the trees in local streets. Write to the local council about their care. Suggest where new trees could be planted.
d) Make a butterfly garden (e.g. Tortoiseshell butterflies lay their eggs on nettles).
e) Clean out a section of stream or build a frog pond.
f) Think of ways of saving an old wall and all the plants, mosses, lichens and other plants growing on it.

Useful apparatus

Plastic gloves, gardening and other tools (depending on what work is being done and if rubbish is being cleared as part of it)

Not all science that young children can do necessarily involves comprehensive topics. Some very small-scale pieces of work can be equally valuable, and it helps if children are used to counting, measuring, sampling and working out ways of solving problems. Also, if time is short, a brief investigation can be done with reasonable ease. This could, if handled properly, teach the children how to carry out simple research and to record the results in a clear and sensible way.

Activities and experiments

1 The children can make a bird count.
a) Count the birds seen in a particular area (such as the school playground) over a timed period. This can be compared with either a count of the same duration made in another area or with a count done in the same place, but at a different time of the day or under different weather conditions.
b) Make a count of the types of birds seen in a specific area at a fixed time. The children need to be able to identify the birds likely to be seen. The table provides an example.

Birds seen on the school field on May 2nd: 10:00–12:00 am					

If such a count is carried out on several days, the children can decide which are the commonest birds of the area.

2 With the gradual loss of suitable habitats, such animals as the frog and newt are becoming increasingly rare in many areas. It would be interesting to find places where they are managing to survive, or even managing to increase. Make a frog count of the immediate environment. Try to involve children from other schools in other districts.

3 Averages – this is particularly useful because it applies mathematical concepts to biological topics.
a) Count the number of petals on daisies. Are there always the same number? Count the number on 10 flowers. Find the average number of petals. How many times do the children consider they will have to do this to get a reasonably accurate average?
b) Measure the hand span of all the children in the class. Work out the average span. Is it possible to draw any conclusions from this? Do tall children have a hand span above average?

4 Making a ground profile – decide on the stretch of ground where the profile is to be made and then on the length. Put in a stake at each end and stretch a strong string between the two, making sure that is is perfectly level by using a spirit level (see the illustration). Using a metre ruler, measure the distance between the ground level and the string. Do this every 20–30 cm so that a plan can be drawn on squared paper. Sketch in the plants in the right positions (symbols can be used). Compare profiles made in several places.

5 Look at walls and fences and collect information about algae and lichens. (The children do not need to identify these by names.) Do these grow only on stone surfaces? Why are some surfaces more prone to growth than others? Does the surface have to be old before these plants begin to grow? Do they damage the surface? Look at trees and find out if algae grow equally well all over the trunk. What affects the growth?

6 List all the animals seen near the school during one week. The children can take it in turns to act as the observer. Include domestic pets as well as wild animals, birds, amphibians or insects. Try to decide why the animals are in the area. Is the presence of animals associated with feeding? Work out some of the possible food chains and see if there is any connection between the visitors and possible feeding habits. For example:

Nettles → caterpillars → sparrow → sparrow hawk
Rose bushes → greenfly → ladybirds → insect-eating birds

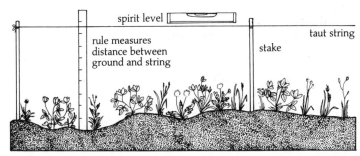

Making a ground profile

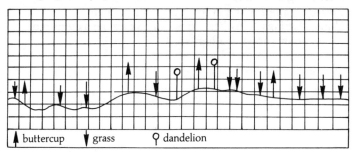

Chart of a ground profile

7 Examples of sampling – mark out a definite area of ground (say a 50 × 50 cm square) and put strings every 10 cm from left to right and from top to bottom so that 25 smaller squares are formed. Make an accurate count of all the plants seen, marking them on a chart. (The guide strings will help.) The children can also call out their finds to a partner using coordinates.

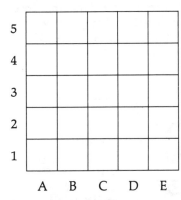

Each cross represents a clover – found in squares A5, B4, C2 and C5

8 Setting problems – these give children the opportunity to work out their own ways of finding the answer. Problems need not be biological, but they should always necessitate experimentation or direct observation. Examples:
a) Find out what sort of food will best attract wild birds to the bird table.
b) What effect does the tide have on shore habitats?
c) How far will woodlice move from the place they are found? (Woodlice can be marked with a tiny spot of nail varnish.)
d) How well are biscuits packaged. Do they stay fresh?
e) Which type of floor covering stands up to the most wear and tear?
f) Which colour attracts the most insects?

Useful apparatus

Tape measures; squared paper; card; string; pegs and posts; wooden metre rules; trowels; clipboards

97

Children like collecting things and with very little encouragement they will pick up stones, shells, grasses, boxes, labels and so on. This enthusiasm can be used very successfully for the start of science projects, but unless the collections have a definite purpose, they will soon degenerate into unlabelled and unidentified groups of objects which may or may not have something in common. This does not mean to say that children's own collections should be so structured that they lose interest in it, but it does mean that they should be given every opportunity to use and display their collection, and should be helped to identify things and to classify them in some way.

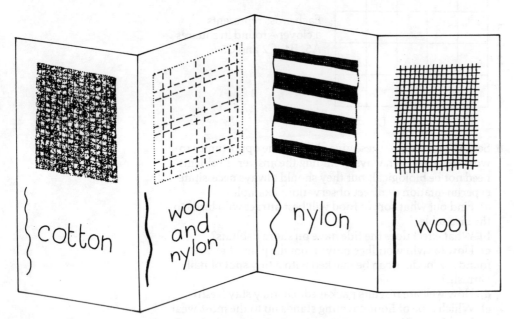

A zigzag book used for displaying a collection

General notes

It is impossible to make a list of all the things that could be collected. They will vary according to interest, locality, opportunity and age, but there is always something worth looking for. These are some of the possibilities:

Leaves (specimens, rubbings or plaster casts)
Flowers (specialized collections from specific areas, but note the rules of conservation in section 44)
Bark rubbings
Grasses
Tree collections (pictures, specimens, rubbings, fruits, etc.)
Fruits and seeds
Food plants
Caterpillars and other small animals
Shore life
Bones
Rocks, stones and fossils
Yarns and fabrics
Tools
Wood or metal objects
Building materials
Paper
Packaging materials
Postage stamps with plants or animals on them
Unusual things (a broken clock; an oak apple; a coloured stone; an unknown feather, etc.)

Activities and experiments

1 Animals in the garden or school grounds – although such small animals as spiders and ladybirds can be kept for a short time, most of this collection will have to be in the form of drawings and pictures. This has the advantage that it can be added to as new specimens are found. One collection I know of, in a suburban school, included sparrows, starlings, wagtails, blue tits, a seagull, wood pigeons, three types of spider, wasps, honey bees, bumble bees, ladybirds, violet ground beetles, earthworms, small tortoiseshell caterpillars, earwigs, woodlice, houseflies, several other unnamed flies, domestic cat, small white butterfly and ants.

2 Some collections are useful for future reference to help in identification. Leaves and flowers can be pressed between sheets of blotting paper and several thicknesses of newspaper. These need to be placed under a heavy weight for some weeks. Alternatively, a press can be made with two thick pieces of plywood and two heavy G-clamps. The pressed specimens can be mounted with tiny strips of tape, or can be placed on card and covered with adhesive laminating sheeting.

3 Collections of younger children will have to be grouped if detailed identification would be too difficult:
a) Yarns – possible groupings are yarns used for knitting, thick yarns, thin yarns, yarns made by twisting several threads together (plied), by colour, threads pulled out of pieces of material, threads used for sewing, smooth yarns, hairy yarns.
b) Shells – possible groupings are spiral shells, flat shells, domed shells, shells in two parts (bivalves), small shells, large shells, black and grey shells, coloured shells.

c) Stones – possible groupings are according to where they were found (on the shore, in the garden, park, etc.), smooth stones, rough stones, stones with holes in them, brightly coloured stones, stones used for building, polished stones.

4 Work arising from collections will vary, but some follow-up work should be done. For example:
a) The children can use the tape recorder to make commentaries to go with their specimens. These can be used with small tape recorders and left with the displays for other children to hear. Here is an example:

> This is a collection of bones. All of these bones came from birds or mammals and were found by children in our class. Number 1 is a bird's skull. You can see the beak and the holes where the eyes were.
> Number 2 is from a sheep. It is one of the bones from the spine.
> Numbers 3, 4 and 5 are rabbit bones. We think that they are all leg bones.

The collection and tape recording can be reinforced by slides and a small viewer. For example, with the above recording, slides of a rabbit, a sheep and a bird could be shown.
b) Packaging – testing the strength of boxes; finding out if packages are damp proof; finding out how easy it is to open a package.
c) Postage stamps with, say, animals on them – finding out about each animal from books; making a card index of the animals (each card can have the name, habitat and some information on it).
d) Tools – demonstration of the tools being used. These can be the tools related to a particular craft. It may be possible to get parents to help with this by lending tools of all sorts.

Useful apparatus

Shoe boxes, match boxes and others for display trays; cellophane; card; felt pens; glue; adhesive tape; pots and bags for collecting; jars for water collections; labels; tape recorder; slide viewer; adhesive laminated sheeting

A TREE CHART – PROJECT SHEET

Name:

Tree:

Location:

Estimated height:

Girth:

Possible age:

Area shaded by tree:

Animals and plants under tree:

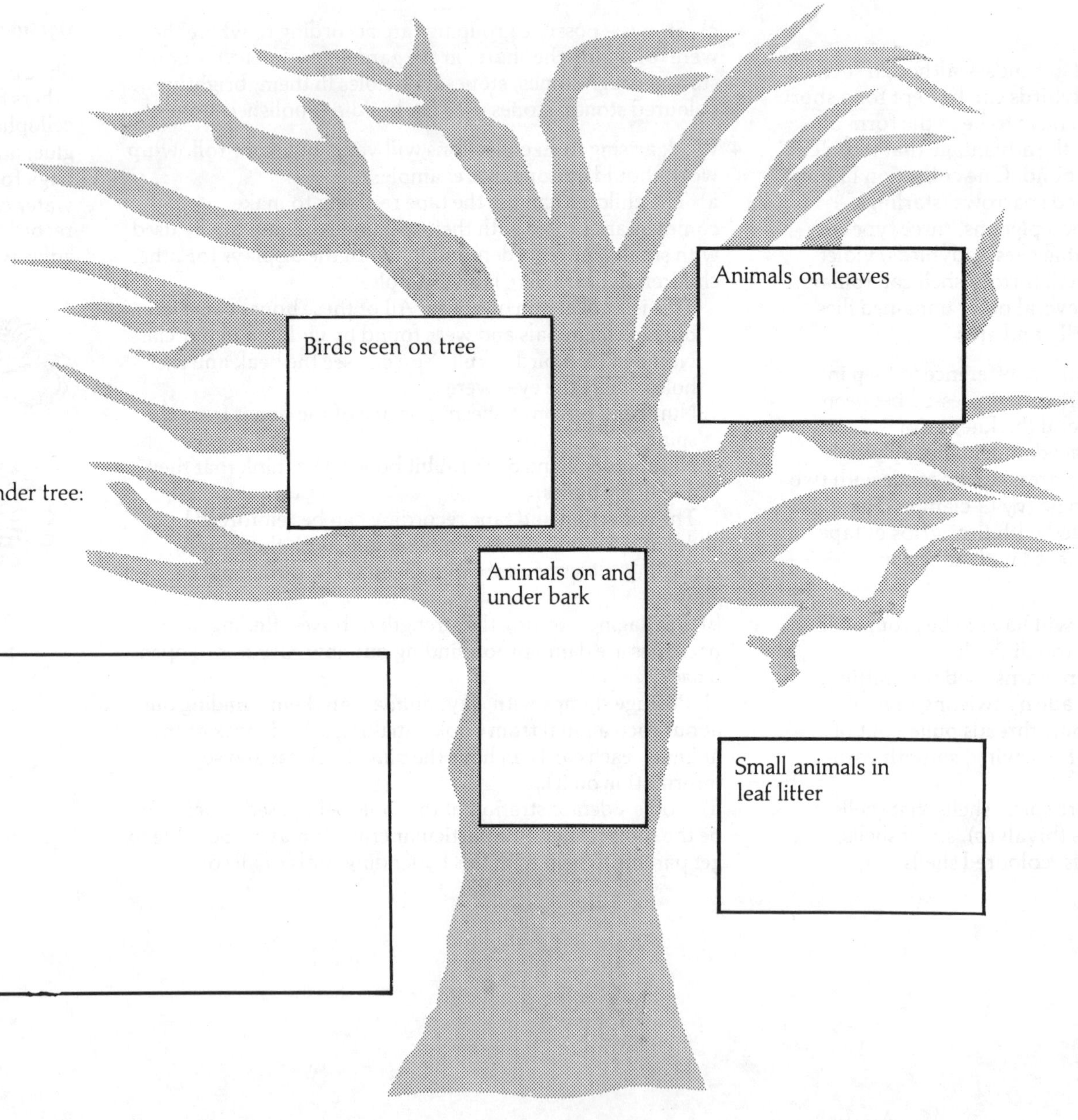

Birds seen on tree

Animals on leaves

Animals on and
under bark

Small animals in
leaf litter

Pictures and drawings can
be stuck on instead of writing

Stick bark rubbing here

Drawing – leaf, fruit

ENVIRONMENTAL STUDY PROJECT SHEET

Name:

Place:		**Type of environment:**	
General description:		Natural or created by people:	
Trees – name, location, number, age, size, condition:	Animals (vertebrates) Mammals: Birds: Reptiles, amphibia, fish:	Buildings, houses, walls, roads, structures:	
		Any other features and notes:	
Other plants (including water plants):	Animals (invertebrates) Insects:	Others:	
	Drawings:		

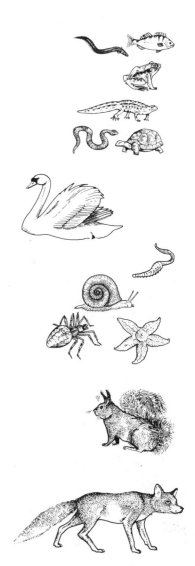

BIBLIOGRAPHY

Action Science Series *Sun and Light* Franklin Watts 1983
Althea *Animals at Your Feet* Dinosaur Publications 1985
Barns, R *Coasts and Estuaries* Hodder & Stoughton
Barrett, J & Yonge, C M *Pocket Guide to the Seashore*
 Collins
Barrett, J & Yonge, C M *Sea Shore* Collins
Bellamy, D & T *Bellamy's Backyard Safari*
 BBC Publications 1981
Bennet, J & Smith, R *Bright Ideas for Science*
 Ward Lock Educational
Benson, A & Warburton, N *Looms and Weaving*
 Shire Publications 1986
Bishop, Owen *Adventures with Small Animals*
 John Murray 1982
Bishop, Owen *Adventures with Small Plants*
 John Murray 1983
Bornancin, B *Small Animals in Captivity* Burke Books 1983
Brown, Rachel *Weaving, Spinning & Dyeing Book*
 Routledge & Kegan Paul 1979
Chinery, Michael (ed) *Natural History of Britain and Europe*
 W H Smith
Chinery, Michael *Natural History of the Garden*
 Fontana Collins 1977
Dempsey, M W (ed) *Rainbow Book of Science* W H Smith
Diamond, Dorothy *Air and Water Activities* Hulton 1983
Diamond, Dorothy *Science with Plants*
 Ward Lock Educational 1988
Drabble, Phil (ed) *Country Compass* AA Publications
Garner, L *Dry Stone Walls* Shire Publications 1984
Gilman, D *Life on the Seashore* Macdonald Educational 1981
Goodwin, J & Jacklin, M *Growing Things in School*
 Ward Lock Educational
Jamilton, R & Insole, A *Finding Fossils* Kestrel Books
Jackman, Leslie *Seashore Naturalists Handbook* Hamlyn
King, S F *Science and Air* Hart-Davis
King, S F *Science for Primary Schools*
 Ward Lock Educational 1985–7

Layton, Dudley A *Old Woodworking Tools*
 Jarrold Publications
Leadbeater, Eliza *Spinning and Spinning Wheels*
 Shire Publications 1979
Leigh-Pemberton, J *Hedges* Ladybird Books 1979
Leutscher, A *Ecology of the Woodlands* Franklin Watts
Mitchell, Alan *Trees of Britain and Northern Europe*
 Collins 1978
Owen, Denis *Towns and Gardens* Hodder & Stoughton
Palmer, Joy *Garden as a Nature Reserve*
 Dryad Educational Books 1985
Phillips, Roger *Grasses, Ferns, Mosses and Lichens* Pan Books
Phillips, Roger *Trees in Britain, Europe and North America*
 Pan Books 1978
Phillips, Roger *Wild Flowers of Britain* Pan Books 1977
Pluckrose Henry *Things to Hear* Franklin Watts
Readers Digest *Butterflies and Other Insects of Britain* 1984
Readers Digest *Traditional Crafts in Britain* 1982
Riley, Peter D *Materials* Dryad Educational Books
Roberts, M B V & Mawby, P J *Biology 11–13* Longman 1983
Sauvain, P *Looking Around in Town and Country*
 Franklin Watts 1982
Science 5/13 *Early Experiences* Macdonald Educational 1972
Science 5/13 *Metals – Stages 1 & 2*
 Macdonald Educational 1973
Science 5/13 *Structures and Forces*
 Macdonald Educational 1972
Science 5/13 *Time – Stages 1 & 2* Macdonald Educational 1972
Showell, Romola *Hedges, Walls and Boundaries*
 Dryad Educational Books 1986
Streeter, D & Richardson, R *Discovering Hedgerows*
 BBC Publications 1982
Wake Up to the World of Science Series *Heat and Temperature*
 Burke Books 1983
Young, Geoffrey *Watch – A New Way of Exploring Nature*
 Watch Trust for Environmental Education 1981
Zim, H S & Shaffer, P R *Rocks and Minerals* Hamlyn

INDEX

A

absorption of heat   68
acid rain   94
adhesives   48, 49
air   72, 73
algae   15, 34, 95
alloys   46
amphibians   10, 17
animals in winter   78, 79
ants   18
arch   56, 58, 59
asexual reproduction   28
ash   80
averages   96

B

bacteria   38
barnacles   95
beam bridge   58, 59
beech   14, 80
birds   17, 87, 88, 90, 92
blue whale   26
bones   30, 32, 33, 98
boundaries   80
bramble   12, 81
brick   86
brickwork   84, 86
bulbs   8, 9, 28
butterflies   18, 19, 81

C

camouflage   60
cantilever bridge   58, 59
cartilage   32
castles   84
caterpillar   11, 18, 19, 28, 98
cement   40, 41, 57

chalk   40
chlorophyll   8, 36
classification   16, 17
clay   38, 40, 41, 74
clepsydra   64
climbing plants   8, 66
clocks   64, 65
coal   41
cold-blooded   16
collecting   98, 99
communities   22
condensation   44, 45, 74
coniferous trees   14, 15
conservation   94, 95
copper   46
corms   8, 28
cotton   42
crustacea   22, 88

D

dating a hedge   80
deciduous trees   14, 15
dispersal of seeds   12, 13
display boxes   13
dog   92
dragon fly   35
dry stone wall   86, 87
dyeing   42

E

earthworm   20, 21, 38
earwig   19, 23
echoes   62
eggs   28, 29
elder   80
evaporation   44, 45, 68,
   74, 76, 77

evergreens   14, 15
exo-skeleton   32

F

fabric   42, 43
ferns   87
fibres   42, 43
fish   34, 35, 88
flowering plants   17, 90
food chains   10, 23
fossils   41
fox   38, 91
freezing   78, 79
friction   54, 55
frog   10, 27, 28, 35
fungi   15, 36, 37

G

gerbil   25
giraffe   26
glues   48, 49
grafting   28
granite   40
ground profile   96
growth   10, 11, 12, 26, 30
growth rate   11
guinea pig   10, 25

H

habitat   22, 23, 85
hamster   25
hardness of water   44
hawk moth   38
hawthorn   80
hearing   62, 63
hedgehog   81
hedges   80, 81

herbicide   94
hermaphrodites   20
hibernation   21, 69, 78
honeycomb   66
horse chestnut   14

I

ice   78, 79
insect life cycle   18, 28
insect pests   18, 19
insects   16, 18, 19, 22
invertebrates   16, 20, 21
iron   46, 47

K

kaleidoscope   71

L

ladybird   18, 19, 99
landscape   82
lead   46
leaf litter   80, 81
leech   34
lever   52, 53
lichen   84, 87, 90, 96
lifespan   11
limpet   88
linen   42
loom   43

M

machines   52, 53
magnetism   47
mammals   16, 24, 25, 91
measurement   66, 67
mercury   47
mineral salts   38

misteltoe   15
mole   26
molluscs   8, 41
mosquito   14
moss   90
moths   18, 19, 39, 81
mouse   24
mucor   36, 37
muscles   32

N

nests   28, 80
newt   34
night and day   64, 76
noise   62
non-flowering plants   36

O

oak   14, 15, 80
owl   87
oxygen   72, 73

P

paths   85
pesticides   94
pet care   24, 25
photosynthesis   8, 76
phototropism   8
plant kingdom   16
pods   12
pollination   28
pollution   90, 94, 95
polyesters   42
pond life   34, 35
potato   8
power tools   52
primary colours   60

protozoa   22, 38
pulleys   52

R

rabbit   24, 38
ragwort   90
rain   74, 75
reflection   70, 71
refrigeration   79
resistance   54, 73
respiration   30
rocks   40
rollers   50
roots   14
runners   8, 28
rusting   47

S

sampling   96
sand dune   88
sandstone   40
seasons   76
seaweed   88
seed dispersal   12
seeds   8, 9, 12, 13, 28
sexual reproduction   28
shadows   76, 77
shark   32
sheep   43, 82
shore   88
shore line   88
silk   42
skeleton   26, 32, 33
skin   30, 31
skull   32
slate   40
slug   20

smell   31
snail   20, 21, 86
snow   78
soil   16
soil profile   96
spider   15, 20, 22,
   81, 86
spindle   42
spinning   42
spirogyra   34
spores   28, 36
squirrel   15
steel   46
stick insect   19
streamlining   92
stone   40, 56, 86
stone age   40
stress   56
street names   90
sundials   64, 65
suspension bridge   58
sycamore   14, 80
symmetry   66

T

tadpole   10, 17
taste   31
teeth   25
temperature   16, 68
test for hardness (rock)   41
thermometer   69
tides   88
toadstool   36
topsoil   38
transport   50
trees   12, 14, 90
tubers   8

V

vacuum   72
vegetable dyes   42
vegetative reproduction   8, 12
verges   85
vertebral column   32
vertebrates   16, 32

W

walls   86
warm-blooded   16, 68
water   44, 74
water flea   34
water plants   34
waterproofing   74, 75
water snail   35
weapons   52
weaving   42
wellingtonia   14, 26
wheels   50, 51
whitebeam   14
white light   60
willow-herb   90
winged fruits   12, 13
winter   78
wood   14
woodlouse   21, 98
wool   18, 42

Y

yarns   42